D1162444

LITURGY AND CHRISTIAN UNITY

Romey P. Marshall

President-emeritus, the Order of St. Luke

Michael J. Taylor, S.J.

Assistant Professor, Seattle University, Seattle, Washington

PRENTICE-HALL, INC., Englewood Cliffs, N.J.

TO THE MEMORY OF POPE JOHN XXIII
WHOSE ECUMENICAL SPIRIT OF CHARITY
HELPED CHRISTIANS REALIZE ANEW THEIR
COMMON BROTHERHOOD IN CHRIST

Library of Congress Catalog Card No.: 65-17534

Printed in the United States of America [53782-C]

PRENTICE-HALL INTERNATIONAL, INC., *London*
PRENTICE-HALL OF AUSTRALIA, PTY., LTD., *Sydney*
PRENTICE-HALL OF CANADA, LTD., *Toronto*
PRENTICE-HALL OF INDIA (PRIVATE) LTD., *New Delhi*
PRENTICE-HALL OF JAPAN, INC., *Tokyo*

Foreword

Ten years ago a Catholic-Protestant dialogue such as this book would have been unlikely. Twenty-five years ago, it would have been unthinkable. So God the Holy Spirit works in ever-new and astonishing ways. To Him alone we owe this gracious and marvelous boon—a change of heart and mind that leads brethren in Christ once again, after four hundred years of indifferent if not hostile separation, to understanding, sympathy, and an ardent desire to be one—as our Lord Jesus Christ prayed on earth and continually prays in heaven that we may be.

Both Father Taylor and Doctor Marshall recount the story of how we lost our way together in generations past, how again the light of liturgical renewal guides us back to fellowship and common witness. This story, remarkable in its achievements to date, is not as yet well enough known by many of the clergy and laity. A book such as this—in reasonable compass, readable exposition, and ready honesty both in agreements and disagreements—should be of great value in removing ignorance and prejudice.

Reading these conversations, one is struck, first of all, by the lack of concern to argue or make central the old controversies that divided us—the nature of the Real Presence and the Eucharistic sacrifice, the sufficiency of the Scriptures for all doctrine, the authority of the Church and its ministers. Instead, the discussion focuses on new issues that divide not so much Catholics from Protestants, but the members of each tradition with respect to the true nature and means of worship.

Both authors stress the corporate, rather than the individualistic approach to worship. Both appeal to the necessary complement of Word and Sacrament, and the pitfalls of separating them. Both insist upon an intelligent understanding of the act of worship by the laity. Thus, in both the Catholic and the Protestant traditions there is a primary need for very practical teaching concerning the meaning and relevance of Christian worship. Father Taylor expresses this succinctly in his remark that the liturgical rite and ceremony "should not require extensive catechesis to explain its presence; if it has obvious meaning, it should stay, if it has lost its meaning, it should go." Doctor Marshall reminds Protestants that they "are still fighting battles over practices that are being given up, opposing

408

positions that are not now held, and overlooking the fact that Protestants and Catholics alike are on the verge of a reformation which is bringing them closer together in theology and in practice."

It is good therefore to have these informed leaders and scholars of our separated traditions thus lay bare in simple and straight-forward ways the great agreements. Let us hope that these pages of brotherly conversation will inspire similar meetings at every level of the Church's life, that through a better understanding of what is primary in our Christian life, namely, our common worship of God in the Body of Jesus Christ, may we, by renewing our commitment, also enlarge our unity.

Berkeley, California MASSEY H. SHEPHERD, JR.

Preface

When Protestants and Catholics look at each other's liturgy or formal worship, they are sometimes befuddled; they often misinterpret what they see and hear. They can pronounce harsh verdicts on each other because they seldom take the time to inquire into the what, how, and why that go to make up the worship life of their separated brothers. Or, if they take the time, relying as they do on their intramural manuals to describe the liturgies of their fellow Christians, they often acquire little more than half the picture.

This book, in the first part of each section, is an attempt to project for our separated brothers not only the facts about Protestant and Catholic liturgy, but the rationale behind these distinctive modes of Christian worship. Hopefully the work will clarify positions where much confusion exists. The authors feel that Christians especially show their understanding of the faith during their acts of formal worship; if they would really know one another, they must with honesty observe their brothers at worship.

The book begins with a look at Protestant and Catholic liturgy from the standpoint of the theological "ideal"; it describes theologically what these liturgies in essence are and what they try to do. Next the book investigates briefly the historical development of Protestant and Catholic liturgy; it recalls the good and less than good developments which have marked the evolution of these liturgies in history. Then a word is said about the current liturgical renewals that are infusing new life into Protestant and Catholic worship; having shown that compromise-developments were made along the way, frustrating the function of good liturgy, the authors outline the steps being taken to bring liturgy closer to the "ideal."

For many years now the ecumenical movement has brought Protestants and Catholics together to clarify points of theological agreement and difference. Christians are becoming steadily more conscious of the scandal of their divisions. They want to remove the bias that has clouded their understanding of each other. They want to investigate the Christian heritage they share in common. They want to inquire into every possible avenue that could bring them closer together in a unity which they see as clearly willed by Christ.

In this connection, they ask about common prayer as a means to plead God's intervention in the cause of Christian unity. The possibility of a united Christian liturgy has been suggested. This is a sincere proposal and one that should be seriously considered, for ecumenical effort that stops short of common prayer has hardly begun. The book, then, investigates the unitive implications of Protestant and Catholic liturgy, for the present and for the future. Having seen how Christians explain their liturgies, the authors look at their brother's worship from the critical viewpoint of Christian unity. They put forward ecumenical appraisals of each other which aim at judging the elements discovered in the worship of their fellow Christians which seem to hinder or promote the ecumenical spirit; some fraternally motivated reforms are advanced. Nor are they critical of their brother's liturgy only; they also take a close ecumenical inspection of their own worship. Before Christians join in common prayer they are aware that their own mode of worship must undergo ecumenical renewal; here again some appropriate reforms are proposed. Finally, the authors look hopefully to the future and suggest how Christians can work to bring about unity through Christian worship. The possibility of Catholics and Protestants joining in common liturgical prayer is weighed and discussed.

The authors make no sophisticated claims for the book. It is simply an attempt to speak honestly and forthrightly to each other about a part of Christian life which they view as vital to the realization of Christian unity. It hopes to dissipate some of the misunderstandings which Christians have entertained about the worship of their separated brothers. And if there is a special value in the work besides its open and searching discussion of a most important aspect of the faith, it is the fact that it speaks in direct discourse. Too often we talk to each other obliquely or indirectly; here a Protestant and Catholic have joined together in friendly direct clarification of a key Christian action which they feel can, when performed in a spirit of faith, hope, and love, bring us closer to the fulfillment of God's will for us: "full unity in his Son."

M. J. T.
R. P. M.

Contents

A PROTESTANT VIEWPOINT

Part One: Protestant Liturgy

Part Two: The Liturgy and Christian Unity

A CATHOLIC VIEWPOINT

Part One: Catholic Liturgy

Part Two: The Liturgy and Christian Unity

A PROTESTANT VIEWPOINT

Part One

Protestant Liturgy

Chapter One

What Is Liturgical Worship?

Only in recent years has worship been seriously considered by Protestants as a field for study, despite the fact that Luther, Calvin, and Wesley, founders of three of the larger Protestant denominational groups, were deeply concerned with liturgical matters. The liturgical revival, which began among Protestants as an aesthetic movement designed to make worship more beautiful and meaningful, has, by a process of assimilation of ideas from Catholic and Protestant sources and a serious study of theological doctrine, now reached a point where the liturgy is considered the one great hope for unity in the Holy Catholic Church.

But there is a danger that we may "use" worship as a tool. It is more than that. Those who worship are children of God, and to fail to worship is to deny one's heritage. Therefore, it is inconceivable to think of a Church without worship. Our problem, therefore, is to seek to understand the patterns of worship in relation to theology, history, and the practical life of the Christian. Protestant and Catholic ways of worship must be compared to each other and judged in the light of the Faith as stated in the Bible, transmitted by tradition, and exemplified in Christian action.

Before going further in this study, we must admit that no man is able to speak for what is called Protestantism. No writer should authoritatively declare that Protestants believe certain things, lest he be taken to task for covering too much territory. In the first place, the word "Protestant," as it is used today, has become a synonym for "non-Roman Catholic." In the second place, we often include under the blanket term "Anglicans," who are also Catholic; Methodists, who derive from Anglican sources; Baptists, who claim to antedate all Protestant groups; and several more whose theology does not fit into the classical Protestant pattern. In this book, we will omit reference to Eastern Orthodoxy, which is neither Roman Catholic nor Protestant, but certainly Catholic.

Nevertheless, for convenience, we may use "Protestant" in its popular form to refer to those Christian churches which are not in connection with Rome. "Non-Catholic" may also be used in some connection where it seems to apply, but always with the reservation that its use may be inaccurate. As a Methodist, the writer is very much concerned that Methodism should never forget that in the words of the Apostles' Creed (which we say each Sunday) we affirm our belief in the Holy Catholic Church, of which we are a part.

With these considerations in mind, we may proceed to the task of looking at worship from the viewpoint of one who is a non-Roman Catholic, usually called a Protestant, and who belongs to a denomination which looks with some favor and considerable interest at the present trend toward unity of action and faith, if not of machinery. Perhaps this description would include a large proportion of non-Roman Catholic Christians in America today.

The Church at Worship

The Church at worship is the church fulfilling its purpose in the world. It has no other task, for worship is not something done or said in "church," but a life to be lived in view of eternity. Worship includes the routine of daily living, our jobs, our relations with neighbors and fellow-workers, and our attitudes toward nations and peoples.

Worship is liturgy and liturgy is worship, and both are bound up in the Christian life. Yet there are many who think of liturgy as being concerned only with the trappings of worship, the ceremony, the words that we say in the service, the garb of the minister or priest. Nothing could be further from the truth, for liturgy, by definition, is the "work of the people." That is, the way we respond to God, the working out of salvation received by faith, the tapping of the reservoir of God's grace.

Protestants are only now beginning to understand the word, but they have long understood the idea behind it. Liturgical worship may be simple or elaborate, beautiful in symbolism or bare of all outward symbols. Many of the denominations in American life have in the past discarded much of the pageantry and beauty of the Middle Ages in their revolt against all practices which might tend to encourage superstition. Some also have revived ancient ceremonies but without critical assessment of their value or careful study of their theological significance. Thus we sometimes see the anomaly of a Protestant church building with two sanctuary lights above the altar and are told that they "look pretty." We hear of churches where the Order of Service has been "enriched" by the addition of poems, modern creeds, and fantastic interpolations in word and action which serve no purpose except that of confusing the congregations.

But Protestantism has gone through the period of experimentation and is now ready to advance into the field of liturgical study. Some twenty years ago, the writer was instrumental in founding the Order of St. Luke in the Methodist Church. At first, the emphasis was largely upon ceremony, for young ministers were constantly seeking advice on this subject, and I remember many a talk in conference schools and seminaries where all of the questions were concerned with such relatively unimportant matters as the placement of altar candles, the minister's attire and the correct way to organize a processional. Gradually the emphasis shifted, and now the members of the Order are prepared to undertake serious study of the theological basis of worship. This has been true of other Protestant groups who began about the same time. All seem to be concerned with liturgy—not ceremonial, and this is as it should be.

As we begin this study of Liturgy and Christian Unity, it is important that we state our frame of reference. Liturgical worship is simply "the work of the people." This definition leaves room for a wide variety of ceremonial acts. It does not prescribe a set form of words or of action. Presbyterians who stand for prayer are not less liturgical than Episcopalians who kneel; and Methodists who have adopted the halfway stance of "sitting and bowed" may be accused of laziness, but not of heresy. If one goes to the ancient sources for an example, one is compelled to admit that no single position can claim authority, and if the study is broadened to include the various Eastern rites, it will be found that the varieties of prayer position are indeed numerous.

Neither is liturgical worship necessarily concerned with church architecture. The basilican building gave way to the Gothic, the Gothic, to various other styles—culminating in the utilitarian monstrosity of the Akron plan and the "cow-barn" style now popular. But in all of these architectural styles, worship may be helped or hindered, depending upon the degree of religious faith and understanding.

We cannot claim that any one ritual is necessarily the proper one. American denominations have largely framed their morning worship services upon the model of the Anglican Morning Prayer, finding in its stately form and archaic English a sufficiently otherworld atmosphere to ensure that the congregation will not mistake the worship service for an entertainment. But Lutherans have another pattern, based upon the Catholic Mass, rather than upon the monastic hours. And Presbyterians, while exceedingly unpredictable (like the Methodists) in their lack of uniformity, display good insight into liturgical theory and practice. Baptists may vary to an unusual degree, because of their congregational polity which takes little direction from headquarters, ranging in form from the incoherence (liturgically speaking) of a town meeting to the dignified ceremony of a large city church. The Disciples of Christ, while placing no emphasis upon ceremonial or a set form of liturgy, make Holy Communion, or The Lord's Supper, the culmination of every Sunday morning worship service.

In the face of all this variety, is there a general pattern of liturgical worship in Protestantism? The answer is no. But if we ask, "Is Protestant worship liturgical?" we must answer, "It *may* be." The old distinction between liturgical and nonliturgical churches was based on a misinterpretation of the word "liturgy," for, as we have seen, liturgy is the work (worship) of the people, and wherever the congregation is taught to approach God, to participate in his worship, to pray and sing and listen to the reading of the Bible, to meet around the Holy Table, there is liturgical worship.

A denomination is not liturgical by virtue of its having a fixed form of worship, although it is true that such a form makes worship easier by freeing the mind from speculation as to what comes after what, and from wondering when the pastor's rambling rehearsal of the troubles of the world will be done. But one of the most liturgical services I ever attended was held in a rude little country church, with no altar, no communion rail, and no organ or choir. It was liturgical because it was the expression of the hopes, the fears, the longings of simple souls who did not hesitate to pour out their prayers along with those of the leader, who sang until the windows rattled, and who did not save the Amens for the minister but scattered them through both prayers and sermon with verbal explosions of spiritual punctuation.

Thus, when we speak of liturgy we will need to narrow our definition somewhat for the purpose of this book. Liturgical worship, as discussed in these chapters, centers in the sacrament of Holy Communion; the Liturgical Revival in Protestantism is the name applied to the revival of sacramental worship, worship which finds its focus in the sacrifice upon Calvary and its appeal, not to the love of beauty or of order, but to the hungry souls of men who look to Christ for salvation.

Roman Catholic liturgical scholars find common ground with non-Catholic liturgists in a profound appreciation of the great Sacrament. Despite our disagreement over the number of the sacraments—whether seven or two—there is no question where the emphasis must lie. All of the seven sacraments of the Catholic faith are indeed valuable and Christian, but Baptism and the Lord's Supper are the two which Jesus commanded. "Go and baptize," he said, and thus gave the apostles the key to the kingdom within—the way into the Christian life, the first step upon the road of faith. But the way is long and the road is rocky and we must find refreshment, food and drink, for the journey. This he gives to us in the Supper of the Lord, and with it a Means of Grace.

So it is that Catholics and non-Catholics find a common ground of dialogue when we approach the Lord's Table. We must define our terms, simplify our technicalities, and do all in love; but, despite our minor differences (which are often linguistic) we can more easily talk to each other in this field than any other. If it were possible to break down the barrier which separates us from each other at Communion, there would be an immediate surge of unity in love, if not in fact.

Protestants do not make Holy Communion a daily or weekly act of faith; indeed some celebrate the Lord's Supper only four times a year. But among all of the historic denominations the Sacrament holds central place of reverence. It is upon this framework of love for the Sacrament that the liturgical renewal must build, for, as we shall point out later, the failure of the Reformation Churches to build upon the foundation which was laid by Luther and Calvin in regard to the weekly celebration was the cause of a decline in spirituality and a loss of evangelical fire.

And we must not forget that the same loss in the Roman Catholic Church during the Middle Ages was, in part, the reason for the decline in the Catholic faith, which led to the Reformation.

Thus Catholics and Protestants must recover what they have lost, and one cannot cast blame upon the other. The Catholic Church needed Luther in the sixteenth century. But only today are they beginning to appreciate what he attempted to do for the Church. What would have happened had Luther stayed within the fold, had he not been cast out? That question is often asked today, and no man knows the answer. But a look at the course of Protestantism during the time since the Reformation suggests that, had Luther succeeded in bringing about the reforms he sought (and which are being carried out today), the world might have been spared the years of division and acrimony within the Body of Christ; but, on the other hand, we might have needed another reformation by this time, for sound doctrine and freedom from scandal and corruption are not the only things necessary for a Living Church. There must be periodic waves of spiritual fervor when men are willing to pay a price for their faith. Protestants, after the Reformation, lost their enthusiasm, neglected the sacraments, became embroiled in political activity and intrigue—in short, acted just as their Catholic ancestors had done.

The Liturgical Renewal

The current revival of interest in liturgical worship is not confined to the Roman Catholic Church, although the movement may be said to have originated there. It is growing in all the non-Catholic denominations. One of the fruits of this interest has been the reinterpretation of the duties of a Christian, in the light of our awareness of the Church as the Body of Christ. One of the leading liturgical scholars of the Protestant Episcopal Church in America wrote some years ago:

> In our modern Western culture, with its prevailing philosophy of individualism, there is a widespread notion, even shared by professing Christians, that a man who absents himself from corporate worship of the Church harms no one but himself. Such a conception is just the reverse of the early Christian's approach to worship. Separation from the fellowship meant separation from the Body of Christ. Without each one's participation, the Body was dismembered of a necessary limb, and to that extent its unity was broken and its vital force impaired.[1]

This doctrine of the Church as the Body of Christ is held by all groups of Christians—Protestants, Catholics, and Orthodox. But it has been neglected or forgotten to some degree by all. Medieval Roman Catholics, in their emphasis upon the acts of the individual in private acts of devotion, private confession, and the multiplication of masses paved the way for a gradual decline in liturgical

[1] Massey H. Shepherd, *The Worship of the Church* (New York: The Seabury Press, Inc., 1952), p. 7.

worship, for even in church the pious soul was encouraged, at least by circumstances, to consider his faith as a matter between him and God. With few opportunities for intelligent participation in the Mass, he turned to his rosary and said his private prayers.

Protestants, on the other hand, by their emphasis upon the sermon and eventual elimination of the Eucharist as the principal act of worship, lost the practical illustration of the Church as the Body of Christ. True, they often succeeded in establishing a congregational *rapport* and fellowship which seemed to indicate a feeling of kinship in Christ, but the early Church emphasis upon worship was absent, and many congregations, even today, make attendance at the services a matter of convenience or passing interest. Few Protestants seem to feel that by absenting themselves from worship they are injuring Christ's Body. Too often Protestants refer to a particular congregation as "Dr. Blank's church," thereby expressing their tacit acceptance of the fact that they have little part in the worship and no feeling of real fellowship in the Lord.

The liturgical renewal seeks to make both Catholic and Protestant Christians aware of the need for corporate worship. Not simply, in the one case, of "hearing Mass," but of "assisting at Mass," and, in the other, of actively participating in hymns and prayers, instead of merely hearing an anthem by the choir and a sermon by the minister. In order to accomplish this, the Catholic needs to have the Mass in the vernacular and to make the responses, sing hymns, and listen to a sermon which is more than an exhortation based upon some aspect of parochial duty; and the Protestant service must be formed according to a more traditional pattern, offering more opportunity for real worship. One will become less "formal," with a revision of the Mass to conform to modern concepts of congregational worship; the other will become less free, less dependent upon the whims of the minister and the choir, with the sermon being placed in its proper place, as a part of a well-ordered interpretation of Christian teaching, based usually upon the lesson of the day.

It has been said that Catholic worship is less concerned with the individual and his needs than that of Protestantism. On the contrary, popular Catholic piety is often intensely individualistic, as indicated by the preoccupation with prayers to the saints and to the Virgin Mary for various blessings. Despite the fact that the average Protestant's idea of Catholic piety is very often exceedingly wide of the mark (as, for instance, in regard to our criticism of the veneration of the Virgin as being nothing but Mariolatry), yet it is true that many Catholics go to church from a sense of duty, say their prayers for individual blessings, and, most damaging to the true meaning of worship, seem to lack a sense of the worshiping church as the Body of Christ.

Protestants have little room for criticism, for they have, in their overemphasis upon individual salvation and the doctrine of justification by faith, placed worship in the category of "good but not necessary" things. Certainly we have sometimes lost the sense of corporate worship while yet holding to the very things that would promote such worship. Our Catholic friends are adopting some of our ways—the singing of hymns, our emphasis upon fellowship and friendliness, the use of the vernacular; yet, without the liturgical spirit, they will fall into the same pit that we have dug.

Protestants are in need of some elements which are a part of our common heritage, such as the concept of the Church, as more than the churches; the emphasis upon symbol and ritual as an aid to worship; the recognition of the fact that untrained teachers in a half-hour on Sunday cannot prepare children for life in the church.

The liturgical revival in Protestantism is forced to place much emphasis upon church attendance, for among us the individualistic attitude has made corporate worship optional. But this emphasis must come through teaching, not by exercise of authority. In this country, Catholics are much more faithful in their attendance at Mass than Protestants are in going to church. Despite the common assumption among us that this is motivated by fear, I think that it would be much more accurate to say that they attend better because they have been taught the meaning of the Mass and their obligation to be present at this, the *Service* of the Church. Protestants are engaged in so many activities connected with the church that they often excuse their absence from worship on the grounds that they have fulfilled their duty by teaching a Sunday School class, sponsoring a Scout troop, or raising funds for a new building.

And this brings us to the point of the whole matter.

Good preaching will not build a church; it may add to the number of listeners on Sunday morning, it may give status to the minister, but churches built around individuals are not really churches. If the minister can preach interestingly, intelligently, and honestly, if he presents the Gospel as "the power of God unto salvation" and endeavors, by his pastoral ministry, to bring the teaching of Christ to bear on every situation, he will be living up to the high calling of a Protestant minister. But he will not build a church; for only Christ is equal to that task.

"But Christ is not here," says the critic. "O yes, he is," we must reply, for Christ is present with us through his Holy Spirit, present in the Sacrament each time that it is offered, present in our hearts, each time we bow in prayer. In the words of Evelyn Underhill,

> The real starting point of the Chrstian Mystery is not the memorial of a Death but the recognition of an enduring Life. . . . Indeed, it is the fact of the Life which endorses the sacrificial and redemptive character of the death. In the primitive Eucharist, it would seem that the disciples experienced, in a specially vivid manner, that continuing Presence among them of the living Lord—"working with them" as the conclusion of St. Mark's Gospel says—which is accepted as an established fact by the New Testament writers, and was specially known "in the breaking of bread." The stories of the postresurrection appearances, when Jesus stood at dawn by the lake-side and said to the disciples, "Come and break your fast," or passing through closed doors, appeared in their midst, offered no difficulties to the primitive communicant: they were the sacred guarantees of an experience which might at any time be his own.[2]

It is such a faith as this which will bring about a liturgical revival. This concept of the Eucharistic Presence is Protestant, as well as Catholic, and its emphasis can be the bridge between us.

---

[2] Evelyn Underhill, *Worship* (New York: Harper & Row, Publishers, 1936), p. 152.

Chapter Two

The Development of Protestant Worship

After more than four centuries, Protestants and Catholics have taken a new look at the Reformation and its influence upon worship. What, they ask, was the cause of the divergent views in regard to the central act of Christian worship, the Lord's Supper? Were the Reformers justified in their rejection of the Canon of the Mass and the resultant changes in the liturgy? Was there any justification for the iconoclasm of some followers of Luther and Calvin and Zwingli which resulted in a change in attitude toward the old ceremonial acts and a disposition to do away with all but the simplest forms of worship?

These questions are even more relevant today than fifty years ago, for both Roman Catholics and Protestant are concerned with finding a *via media* between their historical attitudes on worship and the liturgy. The recent changes in the Catholic liturgy and the promise of more to follow is causing Protestants to look again at the Mass, seeing it, not as a fixed and unchanging liturgy which has been set down by the Church for all time, but as a living and, therefore, changing, form for the celebration of Holy Communion.

Today we are faced with a new idea in Roman Catholic worship —new to us, at least, for we have not understood the underlying *rationale* of the liturgy. We have thought of it as being totally different from Protestant worship, and have seen in its involved pattern and complicated ceremonial something that is alien to our way of thinking. Perhaps one reason for this misunderstanding is that we have compared the Mass with the average morning worship service of our Protestant denominations. But the Mass is more than that, and can only be compared with our Holy Communion, which, in almost every denomination, is much more ritualistic and symbolical than the service of Morning Prayer.

Let us look at the worship of the Church, the Catholic Church of the West, in Luther's time, and see what it was that he sought to change in its worship.

Luther had, at first, no quarrel with the Church, as he conceived it. He knew that there had been reform from within, as well as corruption from without. He knew, perhaps, what we Protestants are just now discovering, that the abuses to which he objected were, in large part, due to the fact that the majority of Christians in the Middle Ages were not completely Christian, that their religion was almost as much pagan as Christian, for thousands of the presumed Faithful were only just emerging from the thrall of ancient fears and superstitions. It would be many years before they would understand the Faith of the Church.

We must concur with the statement of Dom Gregory Dix as he speaks of conditions in those days and their effect upon the understanding of the Eucharist:

> The population of the empire in the fourth century may have been exhausted and corrupt, but it was at least still intelligent. Where an individual's will and moral sense could be touched through his mind he could be brought to an understanding of the responsibilities of the Christian communicant. The increasing collapse of civilization in the fifth century presented the Church

> with the problem of hordes of immigrant barbarians who though vigorous were for centuries manifestly incapable of even the intellectual exercise necessary to build a stone building larger than a hut.[1]

Such was the situation during the Dark Ages, when the Church was faced with the almost insurmountable problem of assimilating the barbarians and the equally difficult task of preserving the morale and morals of a defeated and discouraged Roman population, to whom the barbarian invasion seemed the last blow to their faith in Christ, a faith which had perhaps been misunderstood as guaranteeing the safety and the perpetuity of the christianized Roman Empire.

One of the fruits of the upheaval in manners and morals, was the disappearance of the old ideals, the loss of educational training. We who have lived through two great wars in a half-century can understand some of the problems inherent in the situation after a great conflict when conquerer and conquered try to learn how to live together. The barbarians were in the majority; they flowed over Europe like a devastating tide, inundating civilization, destroying the old and unable to build a new world.

Catholic historians have pointed out that the Church was faced with an impossible situation in regard to converts. We remember the stories of mass conversions at the behest of christianized barbarian rulers, who thought it only right that their subjects should be of the same religion, and so, for centuries, the mass of the people changed their faith to fit the mood of their rulers; being pagan, Catholic, Arian, as the wind changed.

Says Dix,

> All through the dark and middle ages there was an immense drab mass of nominal Christianity in the background, looming behind the radiant figures of the saints and the outstanding actions of the great men and women who make up the colorful foreground of the history—a mass of ignorance, squalor, and poverty on which no one made any deep impression before Saint Francis. . . . Down to the end of the middle ages this great lay

---

[1] Gregory Dix, *The Shape of the Liturgy* (Dacre Press, 1949), pp. 594-95.

> mass, the product of the mass conversions, was never fully absorbed by the Church.[2]

During this time of chaos, the worship of the Church became changed outwardly, while still retaining the structure and the inward reality. Accretions of ceremonial developed, due to the necessity of teaching through symbol and action the uneducated and illiterate. Often this symbolism ran riot and developed fantastic explanations of the most unimportant details. The reader of Durandus' famous book on the symbols of the Church is soon lost in the forest of fanciful explanations of ceremony, art, and ecclesiastical garments. Such use of symbolism was characteristic of the Middle Ages.

In Luther's time abuses in the administration of the Church were added to the elaboration of ceremony, and, although the Reformer did not at first emphasize these problems, they entered into later criticisms, and the theological problems which arose out of misunderstandings of the purpose of the Mass soon loomed large in the discussion.

Joseph C. McClelland makes the pertinent observation that none of the reformers began by making a break with the Church, even with the Pope.

> By this time the whole of Europe was ringing with reform; by this time there were translations of the Bible in the vernacular; by this time there were creeds and confessions and catechisms expressing Lutheran and Reform beliefs: but by this time there was as yet no Roman Catholic Church in our modern sense.[3]

McClelland goes on to argue that the *Roman* Catholic Church arose out of the protest against Protestantism, and that the reformers made it clear that they considered themselves to be engaged in purifying the Catholic Church, therefore that they were Catholics. "They considered," he says, "that the face of the Church

---

[2] Dix, op. cit.

[3] Joseph C. McClelland, *The Reformation and Its Significance Today* (Philadelphia: The Westminster Press, 1962), p. 92.

had become obscure, painted over by 'religious cosmetics'—human traditions and innovations of mere religiosity. So they rubbed these off, letting the true face of the Church become visible again." [4]

Whether or not they were right in their belief, it is certain that they so believed. And many Protestant historians contend that the split in the Church really came after the Council of Trent, when the reformers among the old-line Catholics, who included French and Spanish bishops, were outmaneuvered and outvoted by the Italian party. After this, the movement of reform died down, although the Council of Trent had made reforms that were badly needed.

Luther did not, at first, seek to alter the Mass in drastic fashion. He did think, however, that the medieval teaching regarding the sacrifice of the Mass was productive of superstition and confusion and for this reason sought to eliminate certain elements which seemed to encourage these developments.

Before the Reformation the Mass had become a sacred pageant, a sort of miracle play. The average man of the time, if he went to Mass, went to watch, not to listen, much less to participate. The modern Roman Catholic phrase "assist at Mass" was, it seems, little understood and forgotten, if it was ever known. It was sufficient, according to popular thinking (but not according to Catholic doctrine), to arrive at church at the moment when, signaled by the ringing of the bell, the sacred Host was held high for adoration. The ancient Catholic doctrine that the Eucharist was a sacred meal, partaken by the people of God, had been neglected and perhaps forgotten. Now the liturgy was no longer the "work of the people," but a spectacle which, to the ignorant, was a magical act by which the priest imprisoned Christ in a wafer and held him up to be adored.

It was seldom that any but the priests communed, for so conscious had men become of the stupendous miracle of the Mass that fear had replaced love and the consecrated Host was popularly supposed to be dangerous to those who were unworthy. Not more than six hundred years had elapsed before communions had almost

[4] McClelland, op. cit.

ceased among the laity, and Holy Communion had become almost a clerical and monastic monopoly. For a time the tide changed, but still there was disagreement over whether lay communions were greatly to be desired. Such confusion was, no doubt, engendered by the fear of unworthy communions, such fear arising from the very apparent lack of understanding among the laity.

It was during those years between the fifth and the thirteenth centuries that the ancient custom of linking communion and offering was allowed to lapse. No longer did the communicant come to the altar, bringing with him his own offering of bread and wine to be consecrated, for in the years when few communicated, the offertory procession had come into the hands of the clergy, and the layman no longer had a part in the very action which was particularly his own—the *liturgy*. Thus he was accustomed to sit, or stand, and watch, while the priest recited words that were seldom understood or even heard. Perhaps it was only as the celebrant held high the Host that the congregation felt any sense of participation, and this one moment became, for them, the Mass.

As time went on, these unfortunate changes (made almost inevitable by circumstances) set the stage for the reformation which began much later, a reformation which cannot be limited to the efforts of Luther, Calvin, and Zwingli, but which included the earlier attempts of Catholic reformers, and later work of such men as Peter Martyr, John Knox, and Thomas Cranmer in England.

Unfortunately, in seeking to change the pattern of clerical monopoly in the Mass, the Reformers failed to accomplish their purpose of keeping the Eucharist as the central act of worship, and the service became in most cases a form of prayers, praise, reading from the scripture, and sermon, with only occasional celebration of the Mass (which had by this time lost its ancient title, a title which, like many such words, meant almost nothing apart from the action and was based on the phrase "Ite missa est," "Go the mass is finished"). This, as Dix points out, was the ancient service for the Catechumens.

One must agree with Dix that orthodox protestantism in the sixteenth and seventeenth centuries had the general purpose of stimulating devout emotions and reactions in the minds and hearts of the worshipers to the thought and memory of the passion and the atonement, thus practically excluding all other aspects of the Christian redemption.

Protestant worship began to discard the Liturgy, which is properly that of the Eucharist, in favor of a service which was no more than a form of instruction, designed to rouse the proper emotional and mental response. This was not new, for Catholics had become accustomed to the practice of using the Liturgy as a framework upon which to hang their personal and private prayers and meditations. It is interesting to note that this error has persisted to this day most in Roman Catholic worship, despite the efforts of Catholic liturgists and theologians to foster proper liturgical participation, and the average Protestant service suffers from much the same trouble, except that, in frankly admitting that they ordinarily emphasize the Mass of the catechumens and reserve the Eucharist to periodical celebrations, they have saved themselves from some of the ambiguity of the situation. But Protestants have suffered a tremendous loss in thus relegating the Supper of the Lord to an occasional place in their worship.

Further consideration will be given to this problem in a later chapter, but it is important to hold in mind this fundamental difficulty which plagues us. Luther and Calvin both believed in the centrality of what we call the Lord's Supper, or the Eucharist. They sought to make it the "regular" service on the Lord's Day, but their followers were satisfied by the type of worship which appealed to the mind and emotions.

There was no great liturgical renewal coming out of the Reformation, although the implications of the reformers' position lent power to later movements of liturgical reforms. It would be left to the Liturgical Movement of the 19th and 20th century to build upon the foundation, and we must give credit to the Roman Catholic Church for initiating this movement.

Yet Luther and Calvin were not insensitive to the problems and opportunities of worship. Luther, at first, seemed well satisfied with the Mass, as it was, conceding that it derived from ancient Christian practice which, in turn, came from the Lord's Supper as constituted by Christ. He sought to reform the Mass, not to do away with it, to bring it back to its original intention even though he might not, at first, wish to change its form.

Both men saw the Lord's Supper as, originally, a simple act of communion. Elaborate ceremonies, initiated in an effort to help the unlearned, were of little benefit and might obscure the act of devotion. Luther would later curtail ceremonies in the interest of simplicity, but he was not anxious to abolish them, and he held faithfully to the central *action* which Jesus had placed in the framework: the taking up of the bread and wine should be retained, prayers should be said. Other elements were of some importance but of less significance.

After the Reformation, the followers of Luther curtailed the Canon of the Mass on various grounds, thus abbreviating the service and leaving out elements which many liturgical scholars feel should not have been omitted. But Luther would have answered that in his day the Mass had become a sacrificial act of propitiation by which men sought to please God and obtain benefits. Perhaps he was right in taking a drastic step to avoid any tendency to superstition and to encourage the revival of the ancient doctrine of the Lord's Supper as a thanksgiving for the Gift of God already given.

During the next three hundred years, Protestantism continued to emphasize its criticism of the Roman Mass. The effect was to further depreciate the place of the Lord's Supper. Continually arguing against the danger of superstition in the Mass, it gradually lost the earlier faith in the Eucharist, and the salutary efforts to purge the service from accumulated fancies and elaboration eventuated in the production of a form which had little except the memorial aspect. Receiving Holy Communion became the act of man, an act which had for its purpose only the solemn pledging of allegiance to God—which, while laudable in extreme, was not the whole purpose of the Sacrament, as instituted by Christ.

If the Mass has become to many Catholics only a required attendance upon a ceremony during which one might meditate upon Christ's sufferings and his sacrificial death, instead of a joyful acceptance of God's gifts and a willing participation in the "work of the people," Protestants cannot afford to be too critical, for they have suffered a like decline in liturgical understanding and participation. By making Holy Communion an occasional office we have either set it aside as such a tremendous act that the people have been hesitant to avail themselves of its benefits, or we have made it so common and so apparently routine that it has no significance.

In many historic Protestant communions the Eucharist is not a part of the ordinary service, but something added at the end. Some years ago it was common to hear the announcement from the pulpit, "Following the service, we will conduct the Lord's Supper. All who can, please stay." Fortunately such announcements are rare today, and most of the major denominations have revised their Rituals to provide a separate and complete service of Holy Communion, suggesting that this should properly be the order for each Sunday.

But during the years of estrangement of Catholics and Protestants, the Liturgy suffered from too little understanding on both sides. Among Anglicans, who usually do not consider themselves to be in the mainstream of Protestantism, but to be Catholics, the service of Morning Prayer, derived from the monastic *matins,* took the place of the Eucharist in the affection of the people, and for many years communion was rare among the laity. It was left for John Wesley and the later Oxford Movement to attempt to restore frequent communion and to bring back the idea of lay participation in the Liturgy.

Although, as I have said, Anglicans, in general, do not consider themselves to be a part of the Protestant movement *per se,* yet they must be considered in this discussion as non-Roman Catholics; furthermore, because of the influence of the *Book of Common Prayer* upon the English speaking world, and the fact that almost all Protestant liturgies are based upon, or derive some elements from, its matchless language and essentially Catholic outlook, it could not be omitted from any discussion of non-Roman worship.

This is not to say that the Prayer Book is without fault; indeed, as we shall see later, it is much in need of revision in the light of modern research into the Liturgy.

The Anglican Church is both Catholic and Protestant, according to most authorities, and is considered by its theologians to be a bridge between the two positions. Its liturgy contains traces of both emphases, being a compromise in its original form and having been further complicated by various revisions.

The history of the *Book of Common Prayer* is well known, but may be summarized in the words of George Hedley:

> The Reformation in England, under the leadership of Archbishop Cranmer, worked a number of positive, if not critical, changes in the worship usages of the English Church. All services were required to be said in English, a revolutionary departure from the medieval custom. The Mass, now described as "The Lord's Supper, or Holy Communion," was much shortened and simplified. The most far-reaching change of all, however, resulted from Cranmer's creation of the offices of Morning and Evening Prayer, by combining for the former the materials of the older services of Matins, Lauds, and Prime, and for the latter, Vespers and Compline. What happened was that these services, rather than the Holy Communion, became in time the regular ones for general lay attendance; and so they set the pattern for the standard Sunday worship of the English-speaking world.[5]

Here again we see the influence of the Synagogue upon worship in Protestant tradition. Influenced, no doubt, by the monastic worship and the reaction of the common people against the elaboration of the Mass, the English reformers, in their attempt to get back of the Middle Ages, did not go far enough.

At the time of the First Prayer Book, the need was for a liturgy which would allow the people to fulfill their function as the worshiping community, along with the priest. To do this, it was necessary to translate the Mass into English, and to do away with the confusion occasioned by the multiplicity of missals. It is said that there were two hundred or more different printed missals in circulation in the year 1549.

One of the effects of the revision and translation was to give the people a Book of Common Prayer which was actually what it claimed to be, a book which could be used by the people for their worship as a community. Holding that small volume in their hands, they were able not only to follow the priest, but to participate in

[5] George Hedley, *Christian Worship* (New York: The Macmillan Company, 1953), pp. 19-20.

the service after the ancient fashion. Unfortunately, because of many hindrances, such as the resultant controversy between the government and those opposed to it, the change of rulers, the persecution of Protestants by Queen Mary and the hardships inflicted upon Catholics by Queen Elizabeth, added to the normal inertia of uneducated and ignorant people, the Prayer Book was long in coming into general use. Before that happened, it was to be revised in 1552, in an effort to satisfy the Puritan critics, and, ten years later, a final revision made few changes and gave the world the *Book of Common Prayer* which still endures.

Perhaps the most important contribution of the Prayer Book was the office of Morning Prayer, made up of elements from the ancient choir offices, as said by the monks each day. Now the congregation was given a part in worship that it had not had for centuries. English-speaking Christians became used to active participation in a service, which, while it was not the Mass, and therefore not complete liturgically, was an approximation of the synaxis of the early Church, the preparation of the catechumens and the teaching hour of all believers.

Unfortunately, the very excellence of Morning Prayer became a hindrance to liturgical worship, for "liturgy" is more than a form to be followed and must be made up of all the elements of the ancient Mass; antecommunion cannot take the place of Communion. The new emphasis upon the beautiful and reverent service of prayer and instruction, with its heritage of synagogue and cloister worship, did nothing to restore the central rite to its proper place in the service. The old lassitude and listlessness came back; congregations at length gave over their part in the worship to the priest and the clerk (who droned the responses meant for the faithful), and the central idea of the reformation in worship, which was that the people should have a part in Holy Communion, should be active participants in weekly or daily celebrations of the Lord's Supper, was lost, and the people fulfilled their "duty" with only a token attendance upon a function performed for them by delegated representatives.

The natural conservatism of the English people made it difficult to change the habits of the past. As in other areas of life, the spirit of compromise characteristic of any national church led to a form of worship that settled down to the lowest common denominator —which, in time, was very low indeed.

We have not space to enumerate the various deficiencies which resulted from Archbishop Cranmer's attempt (becoming more evident in the revisions) to graft Zwinglian theology upon the traditional form and meaning of the Mass. The effort, while amazing, was not wholly successful—to put it mildly. The Puritan influence gained ground as successive editions of the Prayer Book appeared in 1552 and 1662, with a consequent loss of Catholic emphasis, and the Reformed concern with individual experience reinforced the medieval Catholic tendency to make worship merely an act of seeing and hearing. In the Middle Ages the people watched as a priest officiated at the altar, his back to the congregation; now they sat and listened as the preacher delivered a sermon which became longer and longer as time went on.

The English Reformation had won—and lost. The ties with Rome, which had for many years been tenuous indeed, had been cut and the English church was free of Papal domination, but the original idea of the movement had been forgotten by most men. What had begun as an effort to bring worship back to the people, had now become a static effort at holding on to a form which left little room for the worship of the people.

But, most important, and most unfortunate, was the relegation of the Lord's Supper to an occasional service, fenced about with dire pronouncements against the danger of partaking unworthily, and made a matter of government regulation instead of a joyous Communion of the faithful with their Lord.

The Church owes a great debt to Cranmer and to the Book which he produced. No other publication has so influenced the world since the printing of the Holy Bible, no other book can approach it in the beauty of language, and no other attempts at translating the ancient prayers from Latin and Greek have so caught the beauty and reverence of the originals. Criticisms of the Book of Common Prayer can be made on the basis of liturgical and theological criteria, but none can deny that it is the noblest heritage of the English language.

The faults which we have touched upon are the faults of the

time when the Prayer Book was compiled, a time when the vast field of liturgical knowledge was unavailable, a time when theology was more concerned with controversy than with constructive study, and when, in the heat of controversy, positions were taken which hardened into dogmas without sufficient time for seasoning; when, in a word, it was time for change, a time for revolution.

Chapter Three

Protestant Liturgy in Renewal

Following the Reformation in Germany and the establishment of the Anglican Church in England, came a period of decline in worship practice and understanding. We must agree with Bishop Steven F. Bayne when he says, "That gigantic earthquake, the Reformation, opened great schisms between Christians and between our churches; and all too often the line of division was a frontier between these two spirits." [1]

The two spirits he defines as, on one hand, the attitude which sees the greatest importance in an event in the dimension of Time —supreme offering of Christ on Calvary, which happened once

[1] Steven F. Bayne, *The Eucharist and Liturgical Renewal* (New York: Oxford University Press, 1960), p. 10.

and can never be made again, and, on the other, the belief that, while it is true that the sacrifice of Christ was an event in time, it is also an eternal truth about God. The Lord Jesus is not dead. Therefore, according to this second spirit in the Church, the memorial of the Supper is more than remembering One who died a long time ago, but is an eternal offering which may be re-presented on every altar, every day, "but which is, first of all, outside Time itself."

And he goes on to say,

> Men to whom the action of God in Time was most precious and meaningful looked with suspicion at the devotion and life of others nurtured in a sense of Eternity. "Your sacrament is nothing; it asks nothing of your moral earnestness." And then from the other side came equally harsh charges: "You make of the Eucharist a purely subjective commemoration. All depends on you and your sincerity. You act as if Jesus were a good, dead man whose only ministry now is in the effectiveness of your recalling of Him."[2]

There are dangers in both spirits. When we think only of the wonder of the Mass, of a miracle which we believe takes place upon the altar, when we become content to see and hear, as did the Christians of the Middle Ages, then we lose sight of the greatest miracle of all—that God through Christ gave himself for us and therefore we must give ourselves for him and for our brethren.

And, on the other hand, in our attempt to relate the Lord's Supper to our lives without emphasizing the element of miracle and mystery, we run into the danger of making salvation depend upon our own worthiness, and thus may lose sight of the work of God.

These are the tensions in Protestantism today, as in the time of Luther and Cranmer. Both interpretations exist within the framework of Anglican, Lutheran, and Reformed churches. Indeed, both may exist within the minds of devout men who, pulled between the two extremes, find it hard to come to a decision.

Protestants often fail to realize that there was a time, following the Reformation, when the spiritual element in their movement

---

[2] Ibid.

was overshadowed by the struggle for political power, and the fever of controversy. Positions which might have been compromised in quiet discussion and prayerful meditation became hardened in the cement of orthodoxy. The Council of Trent made many reforms in the life of the Church, but it was, on the whole, a reaction to the Reformation, and it is true in religious controversy, as well as in physics, that to every action there is a corresponding reaction. Trent was a step forward in purifying the Church, but a step backward in attempting to refute Protestant positions which were often essentially Catholic, but which in some cases had been exaggerated by the heat of polemical battle.

Thus it was that, for some years, the Protestant movement was too much concerned with building a theology and a mode of worship consistent with it, to bother with missionary activity, or to study the principles which it had enunciated in the beginning. Opposition begets opposition, and Catholic and Protestant ranged against each other in a battle which to us today seems unduly harsh and acrimonious. Losing the anchor of Church authority, the learned and unlearned Protestants set out to sail the ocean of Biblical interpretation and church administration—only to find that after slipping anchor they had lost their compass.

The proliferation of sects, the increase of enthusiastic doctrines based upon fanciful interpretations, these were unwanted and unexpected fruits of the Reformation, for the Reformers had meant to change men's hearts and thus their lives within the framework of the Church. They had not intended either to discard the Traditions of the Fathers or to base their theology on subjective thinking. In giving wide circulation to the Holy Bible in a day when the Catholic Church had only just begun to make it available to the people, they made it possible for the unlearned to read for themselves what they considered not so much God's Word as *God's Words*—words that might be taken out of context, applied to any sort of situation. Because of the neglect of Biblical teaching in the medieval church, the common people had no basis of evaluation or criticism. Therefore, strange doctrines blew like sparks all over Europe, setting afire the imaginations of men.

It was a time of controversy, a time that lasted for more than two hundred years. It was also a time of political upheaval and national rivalry. During this time the Roman Catholic Church found itself losing its temporal power—an event which seems to have been a blessing; but, on the other side, Protestant rulers were taking over churches, tearing down monasteries, and assuming the right to control religion.

What has all this to do with liturgical worship?

Only this—that the Reformation, which had in it the seed of new life for the Church, which could have brought back the simplicity of the early Church in its worship, failed to do so because of external circumstances. Thus it was many years before Protestantism (including Anglicanism) left off seeking power and protecting its own interests against an attack by Rome, and settled down to ask again the question Peter faced on the road from Rome: "Quo Vadis?" Where were they going, what were they doing?

Protestants started with the assumption that the Mass should be reformed. Luther began the work, Calvin carried it on, within, at least, the framework of the ancient rite. But, as time went on, the proliferation of ideas, the lure of novelty, caused various groups to lose sight of the ideal and to compromise in many ways. Theology, mostly polemical, was in the ascendancy. What a man believed was more important than how he worshiped; therefore preaching was of prime importance, preaching that gradually assumed a sacramental character, taking the place of Eucharistic worship.

We cannot deny that there is a sense in which preaching of the Gospel is sacramental, but it cannot stand alone. "This do in remembrance of me," was not said in reference to the sermon, but to the act of worship in the Sacrament of the Lord's Supper.

As Roman Catholics lost sight of personal worship in their concentration upon the miracle of the Mass, so Protestants forgot the importance of the liturgy in their preoccupation with the idea of the individual and his response to God—which, unfortunately, was sometimes equated with his attitude toward the minister.

A contemporary writer has characterized the Catholic and Protestant worship of our day:

> The intellectual tragedy of Western Christianity has been . . . for the most part in being made captive of the philosophies it has created. How often Catholic theology, after the Reformation at any rate, deliberately imprisoned itself inside the formal categories of Aristotle's thought; and even the noblest bondage in the most spacious and lofty of prisons is imprisonment still. We need not wonder why so much modern Eucharistic devotion has the air of nostalgic poetry scratched on the walls of a cell.
>
> But sterile is the word for much Protestant devotion, too—a barren crunching of the bones left over from the medieval feast, as if there were nothing still to be learned, nor any century that mattered except the first and the sixteenth.[3]

I well remember, as a young student of theology, some thirty years ago, my puzzled reaction to a course in church history which passed over the intervening years between the organization of the Church and the Reformation in Germany. In our history books we had been told of the intervening centuries in secular life, but it seemed as if the church historians had agreed to a conspiracy of silence concerning the events of those centuries. Vaguely I realized that something called the Dark Ages intervened between Pentecost and the beginning of the Reformation. But there was little emphasis upon the history of the Church up to that time.

There is a new trend in Protestantism, and much of the credit for this can be given to the Liturgical Movement. Granting that many Protestants seldom use the word "liturgy" and even more seldom understand its meaning, we are becoming aware of the vast gap between the ideal and the actual in religious life. We are seeking to find meaning in worship, and are becoming aware that the Early Church was right in putting eucharistic worship at the center of its life.

The liturgical revival in Protestantism began in the middle of the eighteenth century, and centered around the Wesleyan revival in England. This statement may be questioned, even by the Methodists, who are Wesley's spiritual children, for John and Charles Wesley are popularly supposed to have been interested only in street-corner evangelism. But John Wesley did not engage in "field

---

[3] Steven F. Bayne, *The Eucharist and Liturgical Renewal* (New York: Oxford University Press, 1960), pp. 12-13.

preaching" by preference; he hesitated long before embarking upon such "strange behavior," and only submitted to necessity when for a time the doors of the Anglican churches were closed against him.

The founder of Methodism has been misunderstood by his own followers, most of whom have seized upon one facet of his ministerial character to the neglect of all others. To these the statement that Wesley had something to do with the liturgical movement and was a sacramentalist to the day of his death has the ring of heresy. But to those who have studied the story of his life without the straitjacket of theory it seems obvious that, somewhere along the way, John Wesley has suffered at the hands of his friends.

Wesley was a firm believer in the Real Presence of Christ in the Eucharist, he believed it to be a means of grace by which men were not only spiritually fed, but in many cases brought into converting contact with Christ. Wherever possible, he either celebrated or received the Lord's Supper daily.

The evidence of his thinking along this line may be seen in the following quotation from his *Journal:*

Speaking of a sermon preached on June 28, 1740, he writes, "I showed at large: That the Lord's Supper was ordained by God to be a means of conveying to men either preventing or justifying grace, according to their several necessities."[4]

And in one of the Hymnbooks published by Wesley appear these words:

We need not now go up to heaven
  To bring the long-lost Savior down;
Thou art already given,
  Thou dost e'en now Thy banquet crown;
To every faithful soul appear
  And show thy real presence here.

And in another of these hymns:

Then let our faith adore the Lamb,
  Today as yesterday the same,
  In Thy great Offering join;

[4] John Wesley, *Journal of John Wesley* (Standard Ed., Nehemiah Curnock, ed., London), II, 361.

Partake the sacrificial Food,
And eat Thy Flesh and drink Thy Blood,
And live forever Thine.

However, he made a distinction between the adoration of Christ in the Eucharist and that of the elements themselves: "We freely own that Christ is to be adored *in* the Lord's Supper, but that the elements are to be adored, we deny."[5]

Particularly interesting is Wesley's interpretation of the "uses" of the Sacrament (if that phrase be permissible). In describing another of his sermons (a frequent entry in his *Journal*), he reported:

> Saturday. 28.—I showed at large . . . that the persons for whom it [the Holy Eucharist] was ordained are all those who know and feel that they want the grace of God, either to restrain them from sin, or to show their sins forgiven, or to renew their souls in the image of God."[6]

Here is a blending of evangelical and catholic practice that was characteristic of Wesley. Even more striking, and evidently appreciated by the audiences which heard him speak, was this Methodist rendering of Christ's invitation to the lost and weary: ". . . No fitness is required at the time of communicating but a sense of our state, of our utter sinfulness and helplessness: *everyone who knows that he is fit for hell being just fit to come to Christ. . . .*"[7]

But Wesley did not willingly leave any loopholes for the careless Christian. "Yet ought everyone to come to the Holy Communion with due preparation—that is, with solemn prayer, with careful examination, with deep repentance suited thereto, with earnest and deliberate self-devotion."[8]

Perhaps it should be noted here that John and Charles Wesley were both catholic and evangelical, both sacramentalists and

[5] John Wesley, *Wesley's Works* (Bristol), XIX, 87.

[6] Ibid.

[7] *Wesley's Works* (Bristol), XV, 316.

[8] Ibid.

evangelists. Reared in the Church of England, they were priests, founders of a semimonastic Order at Oxford which became known (by their enemies) as "The Holy Club," and facetiously named "Methodists" by those who saw little to admire in the brothers' habits of early rising, morning prayers, Bible reading, and preaching, as well as of their odd practice of giving every available moment of their time to work among the poor.

Wesley's contribution to the liturgical movement has been completely overshadowed by his evangelistic efforts—efforts which were much more startling and, perhaps, at the time, more effective, for the Methodist revival was indeed one of the great religious movements of Christianity. But Wesley, by his insistence upon frequent Communion, filled the parish churches with Methodists, much to the embarrassment of the clergy, who were accustomed to yearly celebrations, as we pointed out in a preceding chapter.

After the death of John Wesley, the Methodist Societies, as he called them, were handicapped by a lack of ordained clergymen, and, as Wesley would not permit unordained lay preachers to celebrate Holy Communion, he had been forced to depend upon the English clergy for many of his sacramental services. Even so, Methodists during his lifetime were taught to depend upon the Eucharist as a "means of grace," and to communicate often. Following the death of the Wesleys, the sacramental life of English Methodism declined amid controversy as to whether the "movement" was to retain its close ties with the Established Church or to become a sect, with its own ordination without connection with the historic episcopate. Eventually, the latter course was followed, and English Methodism settled down, on the one hand, to some imitation of Anglican worship coupled with evangelistic emphasis, and, on the other, to a somewhat formalized evangelism, without the intense sacramental emphasis of the Wesleys.

But, before his death, John Wesley provided the new societies in America with a basis for Eucharistic worship in the slender prayer book which he called, *The Sunday Service for Methodists in North America,* with its ordinal and articles of religion (the latter being twenty-five in number, condensed from the thirty-nine of the *Book of Common Prayer*). Along with the book, Wesley gave advice to the leaders in America, suggesting that Holy Communion be celebrated each Lord's Day and that it should be received as often as possible. The "Order for the administration of the Lord's Supper" was taken from the Book of Common Prayer with a few deletions and revisions. Wesley, who was an indefatigable "digester" of all sorts of books, seems to have made some changes for the sake of change; others were made perhaps to speed up the action and shorten the service. Wesley was not a liturgical scholar, else he might have taken the opportunity to revise the ritual of Holy Communion to a greater extent. But his desire was to make Holy Communion the regular service of the Methodist worship on Sunday. On weekdays he suggested the reading of Morning and Evening Prayer.

All of this suggests that Wesley, in his desire to unite the scattered followers in America after the Revolution and the breakdown of the English Church in the former colonies, did the best that he could under the circumstances. He did not understand the difficulties to be encountered in the pioneer settlements—difficulties which would make it almost impossible to carry on orderly sacramental worship without church buildings, ordained priests, or prayer books.

Wesley did not succeed in bringing about a liturgical revival, and his success as an evangelist overshadowed completely his interest in liturgy and his high concept of the Eucharist. Yet the revival which he started was to bear fruit, years later, in the Oxford Movement. J. Ernest Rattenbury comments:

> Nothing can diminish the value of the Eucharistic witness of early Methodism. At a period when the Sacraments confessedly were generally, if not universally, neglected in the Church of England, the Methodists, through their happy Evangelical experience, observed them with the greatest fervor. No parallel can be found in Anglican history to the immense multitudes of Methodists which crowded the parish churches to celebrate Holy Communion. John Wesley made a declining devotion popular, revivified it with a cleansing stream of Evangelical life. He continually practiced and counseled sacramental worship. His advocacy in association with that of his brother Charles, and their

> fellow Anglican priests, are facts of immeasurable importance, not only in the history of Methodism, but in the Church of England. The founders of the Oxford Movement nearly all sprang from devout Evangelical homes. Who can measure the influence of the Sacramental Revival of the eighteenth century upon their thought? [9]

It may seem that disproportionate importance has been given to Wesley's influence on Protestant liturgy and action; yet no man had more to do with the modern renascence of liturgical worship among English speaking people. Perhaps this estimate of Wesley is colored somewhat by the writer's admiration for him. Modern Methodists seem to have largely misinterpreted his contribution and forgotten his teaching in regard to the Lord's Supper. Today the organization which he founded (somewhat against his will) has only recently begun to regain the love for the Eucharist and the emphasis upon liturgical worship.

The Oxford Movement, under the influence of Keble, Pusey, and Newman, was essentially sacramental, but, after a time, became concerned with antiquarian interests, centering its attention (unfortunately) upon medieval worship practices and architecture. It is to its credit, however, that it attracted some of the most dedicated and devout men of the time, and, without it, the Anglican Communion might have surrendered completely to the influences which always tend to destroy the spiritual life of a State Church.

At the same time as that of the Oxford Movement there arose in Europe a revival of worship among Lutheran, Reformed, and Calvinist groups.

The Liturgical Revival, as we know it, is the product of the last fifty years, but its roots are deep within the history of the Church. Today in almost all of the Protestant denominations there is a turning toward worship as the "work of the people," the response of the faithful to the Presence of Christ in His Church. It is characterized by increased devotion to the Sacraments, enthusiastic

---

[9] J. E. Rattenbury, *The Eucharistic Hymns of John and Charles Wesley* (London: Epworth Press, 1948), p. 150.

interest in the spiritual life, and, as in the case of Wesley, evangelism.

The Revival of Liturgical Worship

From the standpoint of this movement we might well formulate a definition of liturgical worship. But first of all, it would help to consider what it is not.

1. *Liturgical worship is not an attempt to "enrich" the service by the addition of various bits of material which might seem attractive, for one reason or another.* It is said that some twenty years ago a denominational committee met to consider revising their order of worship and found that they were not sure of their purpose or how to achieve it. One lay member, in all earnestness, proposed that a hymn be inserted in the middle of the Communion ritual. When asked why he thought it should be done, he replied that he was sure that the people would need to stand up for a seventh-inning stretch at about that time!

Needless to say, his suggestion was not accepted, but his motivation was not far from that of other members of such committees in the various denominations who have, in past years, based their changes in ritual upon no more valid grounds. The liturgical movement has sought the aid of history and theology in its study of rites. Antiquarian interest should not lead us to adopt elements of dubious value for our time, neither should our search for beauty cause us to forget that worship is not ceremony, but God-centered action.

2. *Liturgical worship centers in the Lord's Supper, the Mass, the Holy Communion,* to use the various names applied to this great Sacrament. To speak of liturgical worship apart from frequent Communion is to forget that Christianity was essentially a fellowship around a Holy Table. Protestants, for the most part, have neglected this aspect of their faith and have substituted for it the fellowship of the social hall. One of the most attractive aspects of the average Protestant congregation is its friendliness, yet this great asset could become much more Christian if it were sanctified by the Sacrament. The *agape* of the ancient Church was coupled with the Sacred Meal; the fellowship around the supper

table was only a prelude to the spiritual communion with Christ and each other in the Eucharist which followed.

3. *Liturgical worship need not be formal.* Indeed, it must not be, for formality is always deadly. Form there must be, but the use of familiar words and actions in our worship do not always denote formality; on the contrary, the more familiar the words and actions the easier it is for the congregation to concentrate upon the meaning of the liturgy. Worship must have form. Even an evangelistic service must have a form, and it is sometimes more rigid than that of liturgical worship, for the latter varies from day to day to some extent, while the so-called informal service may easily harden into formalism.

What then, are the underlying motives of the Liturgical Movement in Protestantism?

It seeks to center the life of the Church in Worship which is not static but dynamic, which is not confined to a building, nor strait-jacketed in medieval forms. It does not depend entirely upon words and music, upon a certain way of worshiping. It recognizes the values in the Quaker silence, the Pentecostal emotionalism, the Calvinistic concept of the majesty of God, the Methodist outreach to the unsaved, the Salvation Army impetus to social concern and rehabilitation, the Baptist idea of congregational fellowship, and the Anglican emphasis upon ordered worship.

And, in these days of ecumenism, it joins in dialogue with Roman Catholics and finds that they have in their way of life all these emphases and more. It is the "more" which intrigues us today, the sudden realization that Roman Catholics have in their worship the background for all our interests. True, we cannot accept all that they have to offer, and we hope that further steps in the *aggiornamento* will do away with some additions which have obscured the face of the Church as it is revealed to us. But we have learned that Protestants and Catholics can not only find neutral ground to stand on, but, more than that, can march together in a common cause of liturgical worship.

Part Two

The Liturgy and Christian Unity

Chapter Four

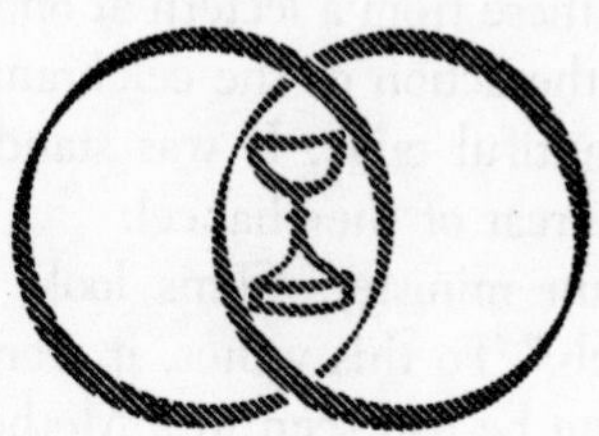

The Catholic Ferment: An Evaluation

No one can deny that something remarkable is going on in the formerly "unchanging" Roman Catholic Church. Those who have studied the trend of events in the last twenty years are not surprised that something has happened; they are, however, amazed at the rapidity and scope of the reformation movement in Catholicism.

In 1963 two hundred non-Catholic guests of the Liturgical Week, held in Philadelphia, found, to their amazement, that they were not only treated with brotherly courtesy, but were invited to express their opinions, to take part in all sessions, and accorded every opportunity to participate in worship—except for one thing, they were not invited to partake of Holy Communion.

At this same meeting, attended by 13,000 delegates and visitors,

Mass was celebrated, not as a spectacle or as something to be "heard," but as something to be done, and the emphasis was upon congregational participation, to an extent which is seldom found in most Protestant churches. A music leader, standing in the pulpit, directed congregational singing of hymns, including one composition often heard in Protestant churches. The congregation joined in prayers in English, repeated the traditional responses in Latin. A layman led these from a lectern at one side and, from time to time, interpreted the action of the celebrant at the altar, which was a plain, but beautiful table. It was standing down front, instead of being at the rear of the chancel.

Said one Protestant minister, "This looks like a Communion Service in our church." To this writer, it seemed much more "informal" than anything he had seen in a Methodist Church. There was little of the pomp which we usually expect. The celebrant took his place in a chair behind the Table, his assistants ranged themselves around it. There were none of the usual ornaments on the Table or near it. Three tall candles stood at each end, a simple wrought-iron crucifix, brought in the procession, was placed in front. There was no Tabernacle, and no sanctuary lamp; only a bare table, upon which was placed, later, the chalice and the containers of bread to be consecrated.

The priest stood behind the Table, in full view of the congregation at all times, and the usual elaborate ceremonial of the Mass was reduced to a minimum. One of the most impressive actions was the procession of laymen, who in street clothes, brought the bread to the Table. Because of the large number of communicants, four stations were established at different parts of the auditorium, with priests and assistants giving the consecrated bread to those who came.

During the Communion, a leader led in the singing of hymns, so that, instead of the awkward silence usually associated with the act in Protestant churches, or the equally awkward droning of lugubrious organ music, there was an air of holy joy and the thrill of full participation.

Admittedly, this was a demonstration of what the leaders of the Liturgical Movement in the Roman Catholic Church would like to see done; it was not the usual Mass, as celebrated in the churches. But such a celebration is becoming more and more common and has the approval of Church authorities.

But the changes in liturgical action, the simplifying of ceremonial, the reading of lessons in English (and in very colloquial English, as a matter of fact), the use of laymen—all these are but indications of a deeper and more radical change in the thinking of the Roman Catholic Church. One had only to listen to the very excellent sermons delivered by the preachers at Mass and to the addresses which were heard during the week, to know that a homiletical revolution is part of the reformation of the liturgy.

What are the outstanding changes which are apparent to a Protestant? There are several:

1. *The emphasis upon the Bible.* There is a quiet upheaval going on in Biblical studies. Catholic scholars are joining with Protestants in an effort to make the Bible real to their people. Despite the common impression that Catholicism is little concerned with Biblical research or with promoting Bible reading, the fact is that now the Bible has become a Catholic best-seller. Many Protestants believe that reading of the Bible is discouraged in the Catholic Church. That was true at one time, but not now. Once it was held that "private interpretation" might undermine the faith of the common people, and that only scholars and priests should be trusted with the Holy Book. Now Bible reading is promoted, Bible classes are being organized.

What is more interesting, perhaps, is that Catholics have ceased to be afraid of Protestant translations and are using them in their study and recommending them for general reading. There is a new translation which is the work of Protestant and Catholic scholars, for the specific use in common services of Protestants and Catholics. The Revised Standard Version of the Bible is acknowledged by many Catholic scholars as the best available version at this time. (A special edition of Protestantism's Revised Standard Version was produced by T. Nelson & Sons for Roman Catholics in Britain in 1964.) Catholic scholars are drawing freely upon the writings of Protestant Bible commentators, and *The Interpreter's Bible,* published by Abingdon Press, is a favorite in some Catholic seminaries and schools.

2. *The changing emphasis in theology.* Roman Catholic empha-

sis in theology is changing in a remarkable fashion. Catholic theologians have, in the past, been too much concerned with refuting the teachings of Luther and Calvin, just as, on the other hand, Protestants have devoted too much time to arguments against the prevailing Catholic teachings. Now it seems that Catholics and Protestants have found common ground in the Apostles' Creed and the teachings of the Fathers of the Church. No longer does the battle rage with so much intellectual (and sometimes emotional) fury around the question of the source of revelation, whether the Bible alone, or Bible and Tradition. There is yet no full agreement, but a sober and friendly discussion is under way.

No one would have imagined, twenty years ago, that Catholic authors would be writing sympathetically and even admiringly about Luther. No one could have foreseen that a Catholic priest would write a book which presented an essentially Protestant conception of the doctrine of Justification by Faith! Or that an outstanding study of the work of Protestant Karl Barth would be written by a Catholic.

"The task of the preacher is simply this, to preach Christ crucified," declared an outstanding Catholic priest recently. In that statement both Protestant and Catholic can agree. Both are now engaged in an effort to do this task, and, for the first time in four hundred years, seem inclined to cooperate in that endeavor.

3. *The emerging layman.* Catholics have, at least in the past, placed the layman on the lowest rung of the ladder. He was necessary, of course, but seldom considered. Today the layman has assumed his rightful place alongside the priest, as a co-worker in the work of salvation. The priesthood of the laity was a cardinal doctrine of the Reformation; now it is often neglected by the descendents of the Reformers. But the new ferment in the Catholic Church has brought this neglected doctrine into prominence again, and the decision of Pope Paul VI to invite laymen as observers at the Vatican Council has given new impetus to the movement, not only to allow laymen more prominence in the worship services, but also to teach them that they are in a true sense "ministers of the Gospel." In fact, the modern Catholic teaching on the lay apostolate goes beyond much Protestant emphasis.

4. *A return to the beginning.* Someone has said that the Refor-

mation began as an effort to bring the Church back to its primitive simplicity and radiant power. That is certainly true. But the Reformation stopped too soon. Theology became polemic, preaching became argument—on both sides of the fence. Both Protestant and Catholic lost ground while fighting each other.

Now we are seeking to recover the lost radiance of the Christian religion. Most Protestants have stopped using the Bible as an arsenal of proof-texts and gone back to studying it as the Word of God for man. On the other hand, Catholics, who had denied the validity of many Protestant criticisms, simply because they were made by those who were on the outside, have now come to a serious study of dogma in the light of the Scripture. In many cases, the modern Catholic scholar has found that much Protestant teaching is simply the ancient doctrine of the Holy Catholic Church. It took four hundred years for us to learn that we were not so far apart after all.

True, there are many points on which we continue to disagree. The infallibility of the Pope is still a stumbling block to most of us, although a careful analysis of that doctrine, as interpreted by the late Pope John's words and actions, would put a different light on the matter, for it seems that the infallibility of the Pope is simply the infallibility of the Church. He is not infallible in his judgment of the weather, political winds, or ecclesiastical whimsies. He gets sick, takes the wrong medicine, forgets his spectacles, like any man. By the time that a Catholic theologian gets through explaining infallibility, a Protestant is willing almost to concede it and go on to something more important, for, boiled down to the bone, the Pope is infallible only in one area—doctrine, and doctrine is decided, not by the Pope but by the Church Councils.

Papal infallibility is a bogey which may soon be deprived of its power to frighten or dismay. Perhaps the next session of the Council will make it clear in such fashion that Protestants may find it comprehensible, or at least imaginable.

But far more troublesome is the question of "Mariolatry," as it is sometimes described by Protestant writers. No matter how it is explained, Protestants can find little merit in the excessive adulation given to the Mother of our Lord. Reverence, yes; veneration, perhaps; and love, most certainly. But Catholic scholars have been fighting a difficult battle for years against the tendency of the common people to go beyond all theological bounds in their reverence for the Blessed Virgin. In vain they explain that Catholics do not *worship* Saint Mary; that the phrase, "Mother of God," is perfectly logical, if not perfectly accurate, for she was the mother of Jesus, whom we believe is the second person of the Holy Trinity—and thus God.

But the answer is simple: Some of them *do seem to* worship Mary. Some give her more honor than her Son. Some never pray except to Mary, thinking that the Mother will, like earthly mothers, wheedle favors from her Son. This, the popular piety of the simple and often ignorant Catholic, is completely outside Protestant comprehension, for we find in it too much of the taint of the Mother-Goddess idea which was borrowed from Egypt and the East.

Is there any sign of modification of this popular and sentimental folklore? Fortunately for the future of Protestant-Catholic *rapprochement* there is. Catholics are reading the Bible more; they are studying the writings of the Early Church Fathers, and gradually the new understanding of the place of the Virgin Mary is filtering down to the people. It will be hard to change the pattern of private piety, which for so long has been centered upon the Rosary, with its "Hail Mary's," and pious Catholics cannot easily give up these habits of worship.

But the liturgical movement in the Catholic Church has turned away from such things to seek a fuller knowledge of God in the face of Jesus Christ. Saints and relics are fading into the background, as priests lead their people in corporate worship of God, as they proclaim the message which Protestants have long thought was their exclusive property—that God deals with man, not through intermediaries, but face to face. The Church is God's Body in the world, and because of this, we must seek God through the Church. But *we* are the Church, we who love and serve him, and every follower of Christ is in some sense a member of His Body, the Church.

Such statements, which sound so "Protestant," have been made by Roman Catholic leaders. If they represent, to any degree, the faith of modern Catholicism, then the ferment within the Catholic Church will have produced something which years of argument could not bring about.

5. *A return to liturgical simplicity*. Catholic worship has not always been liturgical, for so often the people have not really worshiped. Just as Protestants soon forsook the ideas of the Reformers and turned worship into a "preaching service," so have Catholics taken away the work of the people in worship and left it to the priest. Standing before the altar, he has hidden the Bread and Wine which represent the Body of Our Lord, and thus encouraged the notion that he is bringing God down to the altar and imprisoning him in a bit of bread. And while this was going on, what did the people do? Nothing, except read their Missals, perhaps, or say their beads.

That sort of "worship" is still going on in many Catholic parishes, and there are many who prefer it, for it gives them a quiet half hour in which to rest and plan next week's activities, or, perhaps in many cases, to say their humble prayers to God out of a sincere heart. Those who follow the service in this manner may be good Christians, but, according to Catholic liturgists, they are missing the most important part of the Mass. They should have said their personal prayers at home, for the church is the place for Communion—not simply communion with God, but also with each other in the "fellowship of the breaking of bread."

The Liturgical Movement, which has been responsible for most of the reforms in worship in the Catholic Church and possibly for the new attitudes toward Bible study and theology, seeks to return to the simplicity of worship in the Primitive Church. This attitude has contributed to the present attempt to do away with much of the elaboration, repetition, and ceremonial in the Mass.

6. *The results of the reformation*. I have called this Catholic ferment a reformation, and I believe that the word is accurate. If it continues, whether or not all of these proposals are adopted by the Post-Conciliary Commission, there is certain to be a radical change in the worship and life of the Catholic Church. At the close of the second session of Vatican II, Pope Paul VI provided

for changes in worship to begin on February 16, 1964, to include mandatory sermons at Mass on Sundays and holy days and put the administration of the sacrament of Matrimony within the Mass rather than before it. He also announced the establishment of a special commission to revise the missal, breviary, and other liturgical books. Also, Confirmation may be conferred during Mass. In the United States, the Mass is being translated into English and will be used during the coming year. Several excellent English Missals have been published, among them the *St. Andrew Bible Missal,* which emphasizes the Bible lessons in English.

For four hundred years, Anglicans, Protestants, and Orthodox have reacted in one way or another to the theological and liturgical teachings of the Roman Catholic Church. Protestants, in many instances, opposed everything that they thought was characteristic of "Romanism." That they were right in some areas seems to be borne out by the present attitude of the Roman Catholic Church, which now looks with favor upon many Protestant teachings and practices which once they scorned. But Protestants have need of a reformation too, a reformation which would bring about a careful evaluation of their own positions, with the possible result that they would meet their Roman Catholic friends at a half-way point.

In automatically opposing everything Roman, we have tended to lose sight of the true objective of worship; in preaching against Catholicism *per se,* we have sometimes lost sight of the purpose of preaching, which is not argument, but persuasion; not denunciation, but proclamation of the Gospel of love and mercy.

Oddly enough, the new reformation comes at a time when Protestants and Anglicans have almost been converted to some of the very things which the "reformers" would discard. Anglo-catholics have become much more "Roman," in some cases, than the Romans themselves, as their churches add more and more of the medieval trappings and ceremonies. Many Methodist churches in the U.S. have adopted the tomb-altar, instead of the primitive Lord's Table of the Early Church. Most Episcopalians have retained the medieval concept of the chancel, separating priests from people, even accentuating the rood-screen and making it difficult for the people to see the action of the priest. Yet, along with a return to medievalism and preoccupation with antiquarian interests, the Anglo-Catholic movement has brought about a new conception of the reality of the Sacramental life, and has become evangelistic in emphasis. It may be that some "high-churchmen" among the Anglicans will feel betrayed by the "reformed" Catholics, but it is fairly certain that they will be, on the whole, sympathetic and deeply concerned with the spiritual basis of the Catholic reformation.

Despite the efforts made by Pope John XXIII and Pope Paul VI, the Orthodox churches may be less sympathetic to the "new" Catholic Church than the Protestants, for there are many obstacles in the way to understanding, chiefly the doctrine of the infallibility of the Pope (which contradicts the strong position of Orthodoxy on the subject of the power of the Patriarchs, and harks back to the original separation of the Eastern and Western Churches over the question of the authority of the Bishop of Rome). East and West are still in conflict over questions which are based on regional characteristics.

This is to say that the Catholic ferment will spill over into other groups in varying proportion. Some Protestants, preoccupied with their own promotion and programs, will see no reason to seriously consider their own needs, or, if they do, will pay little attention to the underlying problems which are faced by both Catholics and Protestants, except as in the light of certain denominational predispositions. It may take years for the impact of this tremendous upheaval in Catholicism to strike an echoing chord among some Protestant denominations. But such a response seems to be inevitable.

If Catholics, for example, are now more appreciative of non-Catholic positions in regard to worship and are prepared to study Protestant doctrines with an open mind, it would seem that the road to eventual union has been leveled a bit, but there are still some rugged hills remaining. The reform of the Liturgy in the Catholic Church will bring about a new approach to union, it is true. If that reform be matched in Protestant circles by a deep and prayerful study of the meaning and method of corporate worship, there is hope for the future—hope, at least, for an unprecedented *rapprochment* between American Catholics and Protestants. In a case such as this, where cooperation has been almost unknown, any step forward may seem like a long journey.

Chapter Five

Problems of Unity

Is Christian unity possible? We must answer yes, but with qualifications. Complete unity of Protestants and Catholics poses problems that are difficult to solve, at least at this time. Perhaps the greatest hurdle is not theological but practical. If four great Protestant denominations find it impossible to get together, despite the fact that they are agreed on doctrine and united in action, then it would seem that only a miracle could bring about the union of the scattered groups of Protestants with the "Church of Rome," as it has been called. The years of the locust have left a barren field where once grew the fruit of faith and love. If we are to build a highway across that desert land we must first make it possible to live there for a while.

It is this transitional march into the wilderness that we undertake at this time. Those of us who have been engaged in the task for years can remember when we were pioneers, setting out over a dangerous trail, in jeopardy from attack from both sides. But the difference is that now the apostles of good will are being met halfway, and the traffic is becoming heavy on the road to understanding.

Roman Catholic leaders in the ecumenical movement have been quick to point out that the gesture of friendship is more than that; they assure us that the old motive of convert-seeking weighs little today. It is interesting to note that the former emphasis upon this aspect in Catholic magazines is now almost nonexistent. It is true that there are those who still fear that the new attitude toward Protestants is dangerous to the stability of the Church, but their voice is drowned by the friendly greeting of others who are delighted to be able to accept Protestants as brothers in Christ, and Christian ministers, of whatever denomination, as fellow workers for him.

Perhaps the first indication of a thaw in the traditional ice-jam came when Pope John XXIII began to speak of non-Catholics as "separated brethren." Protestants then knew something was happening, for we had been called heretics first, and schismatics later. We had been told that the mercy of God *could* extend even to us, but the implication seemed to be that if we ever got to heaven we wouldn't feel comfortable. I always thought of the old Baptist woman who said that Methodists might manage to get to heaven, but, if they did, they ought to be ashamed of themselves!

But that is all in the past. Now we are not even "separated brethren" to some of our Catholic friends; we are simply brethren in Christ. And that is what we want to be!

Recent books by Catholics have shown the trend toward greater understanding of the Protestant reformation and its leaders. Where once such eminent writers as Eck, Cochlaus, Döllinger, Jansen, Denifle, Reiter, and Grisar saw Luther as everything from a criminal to a psychopath, Catholic historians of the past few years have displayed an amazing breadth of sympathy for Luther and the Protestant movement. In a remarkable book, *Council*

Speeches of Vatican II,[1] the editors have gathered together forty-four short addresses given by the Council Fathers. A few quotations from these will show the attitude of many of the bishops toward Christian Unity. I have arranged these quotations in the form of answers to questions Protestants have long asked, and, until recently, without receiving answers which might indicate a willingness to enter into a real dialogue.

1. *What does the Catholic Church have to say about the Reformation?*

Paul Guyon, Coadjutor Archbishop of Rennes, France:

> It is said that the denominations which have grown out of the Reformation, in their desire to emphasize the transcendance of God, have come to deny the essential mediation of the Church. By saying that, we attribute to them an opinion which they do not hold. . . . Even the famous dictum "Soli Deo gloria, sola Scriptura, sola fide," "To God alone be glory, by scripture alone, by faith alone" does not adequately express what they think. The causes of the Reformation cannot be explained in terms of doctrine alone; there are other causes which have nothing to do with theology.[2]

One who has read widely in Catholic periodicals during the last two years must conclude that the above words express the sentiments of the majority of the bishops, as evidenced by their vote on various matters before the Council.

2. *What is the Catholic attitude toward modern Protestantism?*

Pope Paul, speaking of his sorrow at the divisions within Christendom, said:

> We speak now to the representatives of the Christian denominations separated from the Catholic Church, who have, never-

[1] Hans Kung, Yves Congar, and Daniel O'Hanlon, eds., *Council Speeches of Vatican II* (Glen Rock, N.J.: Paulist Press, 1964).
[2] Ibid., p. 177.

> theless, been invited to take part as observers in this solemn assembly. We greet them from our heart. We thank them for their participation. We transmit through them our message—as father and brother—to the venerable Christian communities they represent.
>
> Our voice trembles and our heart beats the faster both because of the inexpressible consolation and reasonable hope that their presence stirs within us, as well as because of the deep sadness we feel at their prolonged separation.
>
> If we are in any way to blame for that separation, we humbly beg God's forgiveness. And we ask pardon, too, of our brethren who feel themselves to have been injured by us. For our part, we willingly forgive the injuries which the Catholic Church has suffered, and forget the grief endured during the long series of dissensions and separations.[3]

Pope Paul affirmed some points in the attitude of Catholics toward reunion, saying that while there were areas of disagreement, yet there was also the possibility of understanding, and that "we do not wish to make the Faith an occasion for polemics."

In reference to the points of disagreement, Bishop Andrea Pangrazio of Naples, Italy, remarked that not all revealed truths are of equal importance, and continued:

> Some truths are *on the level of our final goal,* such as the mystery of the Blessed Trinity, the Incarnation and Redemption, God's love and mercy toward sinful humanity, eternity in the perfect kingdom of God, and others.
>
> Other truths *are on the level of means toward salvation,* such as that there are seven sacraments, truths concerning the hierarchical structure of the Church, the apostolic succession, and others. These truths concern the means which are given by Christ to the Church for her pilgrim journey here on earth; when this journey comes to an end, so also do these means.
>
> Now doctrinal differences among Christians have less to do with these primary truths on the level of our final goal, and deal mostly with truths on the level of means, which are certainly subordinate to those other primary truths. But we can say that the unity of Christians consists in a common faith and belief in those truths which concern our final goal.

---

[3] Ibid., pp. 146-47.

> If we explicitly make these distinctions in conformity with the hierarchy of truths and elements, I think the existing unity among all Christians will be seen more clearly, and it will become evident that all Christians are already a family united in the primary truths of the Christian religion.[4]

Protestants may find this theory of the "hierarchy of truths" somewhat unusual, but it is significant that it was suggested by an Italian bishop, and it is to be hoped that his interpretation is accepted. Despite the fact that this theory is seldom taught by Protestants in just those terms, it is the basis upon which we unite in a World Council of Churches. We tacitly agree that Anglicans, with their theory of the Apostolical Succession and the necessity of bishops, need have no difficulty in accepting American Lutherans and others who have no bishops, and Methodists who have no Succession! Is it possible that, in the future, this theory may become the basis of unity between Catholics and Protestants?

3. *One of the cardinal doctrines of Protestantism is that of the Priesthood of all believers. How can this be reconciled with Catholic teaching regarding the priesthood?*

A careful study of the writings of modern Catholic writers will show that this doctrine is acknowledged as being a part of the faith of the Catholic Church. Bishop Emile Joseph De Smedt of Belgium, in a speech to the Council, made the somewhat surprising statement (to Protestants, at least) that, as Jesus Christ is "the supreme and eternal high priest," he "actually lives here and now in the layman by baptism and strives to make him share actively in his roles of priest, prophet, and king." Bishop De Smedt outlines three ways in which the layman should fulfill his ministry to the world on behalf of Christ: (1) by living in union with Christ exercising his priestly office by prayer work, suffering, and sharing the eucharistic sacrifice, (2) the layman must exercise his role as prophet in witnessing to the truth, preaching to others through his example, "boldly proclaiming the word of God in his family and social life"; he hears the word of God from his teachers in the

[4] Ibid., pp. 191-92.

Church, but he, through faith, must put it into practice, and (3) "The layman is called to live in union with Christ exercising his role as king. Christ was king of the kingdom of peace, and the layman must work for the kingdom."[5]

This interpretation may seem a bit fanciful to some Protestants, but it is possibly no more so than our own doctrine, for the role of the layman in Protestantism has not been well defined. Perhaps we can learn something from Bishop De Smedt, as he goes on to answer the question, "What are the relations which Christ set up between this universal priesthood and the ministerial priesthood which he entrusted to the pastors of his Church?" He answers that the layman has the right to be "supported, taught, and ruled by the offices of the sacred hierarchy," gaining access to "the eucharistic sacrifice of our redemption and to the sacraments and the graces which flow from them." In other words, the layman is still dependent upon the authorized clergy for the spiritual leadership which is conceded by most Protestants to have been given to the ministers of the Gospel. There is no disagreement here. And he continues:

> Through the prophetic ministry entrusted to the hierarchy, Jesus Christ opens to the layman a sure path to an authentic knowledge and a deeper investigation of the truth of the Gospel.[6]

Here is a seeming contradiction to the traditional Protestant concept of "every man a priest," but a careful study of the writings of Luther and Calvin will show that neither carried their doctrine to this extremity, for each believed that the ministry was necessary. It would not have magical powers, nor would it be the only bridge to God—a man need not be lost for lack of a priest to shrive him, but neither would he live up to his Christian duty if he rejected the ministrations of the pastor or priest.

There is no doubt that the liturgical renewal in the Catholic Church has de-emphasized the former teachings of the priestly function as mediator between God and man. Modern Catholics do not stand in awe of the priest as their fathers did, but they

---

[5] Ibid., pp. 39-43.
[6] Ibid.

seem to accept him as a friend and minister of the Gospel—if I may use that favorite Protestant term.

4. *Has there been a change in the idea of the Church as a world power?*

Cardinal Valerian Gracias, archbishop of Bombay, India, calls attention to the need for clarification of the role of the Catholic Church in the world:

> In those areas where Christians are the majority the Church is accused of wanting to rule the State. In non-Christian regions the Church is often treated as a State within a State. I do not mean to suggest, much less affirm, that this is the fault of the Church, but frequently it is the fault of Christians who want to be "more Catholic" than the Pope. . . .

Quoting Cardinal Newman's question, "But of what value is growth in numbers without a corresponding moral manifestation of the community?" he says, "The Church does not exist to dominate the world but to serve the world." Then he concludes his remarks by asking what would be the image of the Church which would be shown to the world by the Council:

> Will it be the image of a Church always on the alert to smoke out errors and heresy so she can condemn them? Will it be the image described by G. K. Chesterton, the English apologist; "The divine chariot flies thundering through the ages; the dull heresies sprawling and prostrate?" Will it be the image of the Church as Mother and Teacher? [7]

5. *It seems to most Protestants that the average Catholic looks upon attendance at the Mass as a duty rather than as an opportunity for worship. Is this true?*

Perhaps it is, to some extent. Certainly Catholic students of the liturgy frequently criticize both laymen and priests for their lack of appreciation of the real meaning of the Mass—as the worship

---

[7] Ibid., p. 287.

of the people. John H. Miller, C.S.C., editor of *Yearbook of Liturgical Studies,* and a member of the papal commission on the revision of the liturgy, writes in the 1963 issue:

> What is most important, however, is that the saving event of the redemption itself becomes present. The Lord instituted the sacraments—the Eucharist in the first place—to make present his original unique salvific act. At each feast of the liturgical years, specifically in the celebration of the Mass, we do not merely behold a picture of our heroic Savior, nor hear a lesson in Christian doctrine, but rather we experience a vivid and real actualization of Christ in his eternally permanent act of redeeming mankind, gathering and forming men into his Father's family, infusing into them the life of his spirit.
>
> What an incredible event takes place in the liturgy! We go through Christ's redemptive work, we re-experience his transfiguring paschal mystery. . . .
>
> But what kind of Mass do we usually find? Instead of instructing students in the profoundest meaning of the Mass for the Christian life and providing them with a celebration that is truly warm, vital, and inviting, we force them to attend.[8]

He is here speaking of conditions in some Catholic educational institutions, but it would seem that the criticism may apply to much of the parish worship of yesterday. But he enlarges the scope of his remarks by saying:

> How many Catholics today have no other idea of the Church year than possibly midnight Mass on Christmas, receiving ashes on Ash Wednesday, making the way of the cross on Good Friday, joining in the Easter parade and, of course, making the nine First Fridays?[9]

This caustic criticism may provoke an "Amen" from Protestants who have observed the careless attitude of some Catholics, but it might well be applied, in other words, to ourselves, for how many Protestants have no idea of the Church except that it is a good thing to belong to, and no conception of worship other than of

---

[8] John H. Miller, in *Yearbook of Liturgical Studies* (Notre Dame, Ind.: Fides Publishers, 1963), IV, 28.

[9] Op. cit., p. 29.

fellowship and the bored endurance of a sermon which is often aimed at those who are not in the line of fire?

Father Miller quotes from the Liturgical Constitution of 1963, the official statement of the Council regarding the need for training in worship:

> It is necessary that the faithful come to the sacred liturgy with sound dispositions of soul, that they join their minds to its voice, and that they co-operate with grace. . . . Therefore pastors must not only see that the laws for valid and lawful celebration be observed in the liturgical service, but they must also see that the faithful participate in the services knowingly, actively, fruitfully.[10]

Such is the outlook of modern Catholicism, as it assumes a position regarding liturgical worship which could well have been taken by the Reformers, but which, we must not forget, was the ancient teaching of the Catholic Church.

Perhaps the greatest barrier to understanding on the part of Protestants is that we have not clearly understood the revolution that is going on in Roman Catholicism. We are still fighting battles over practices that are being given up, opposing positions that are not now held, and overlooking the fact that Protestants and Catholics alike are on the verge of a reformation which is bringing them closer together in theology and in practice.

It is true that there are many things to which we can still object. We cannot, for instance, become enthusiastic over some of the practices of popular piety, such as the excessive veneration of the saints, the love for medals, saccharine pictures of the Holy Mother and almost terrifying depictions of the dying Christ. We find little to admire in gaudy statues of the Holy Family, and it is hard for us to appreciate the popularity of Novenas. Some Protestants can still see, or think they see, evidence of superstition in the use of the sign of the Cross, and wonder why it is necessary for the congregation to genuflect upon entering the church.

But the Catholic Church is not tied to these peripheral manifestations of medieval piety, and priests and laymen are voicing

---

[10] Op. cit., p. 31.

similar criticisms to those we have made. It is probable that within a few years these practices will have vanished, for they are not a part of Catholic doctrine and most of them are merely permitted, not encouraged.

It is well for us to remember that we should not throw stones, for we are not without sin. Perhaps my colleague, Father Taylor, will have opened the eyes of Protestant readers to some of our faults which loom much larger to those on the outside than to us who have lived all our lives among them.

Papal Infallibility and Power

Perhaps the greatest obstacle to unity, in the minds of the laity of the Protestant Churches, is the question of the primacy of the Pope, the bishop of Rome. No matter how well-organized our denominations, we shudder at the thought of the vast power exercised by the Holy Father, and the average Protestant would have said (a few years ago) that the Papacy was the most dangerous threat to religious freedom. The doctrine of infallibility, as explained by anti-Catholic polemics, seems utterly fantastic and indefensible.

But today we are inclined to look with more favor upon the idea of a supreme pontiff, since we have learned that the infallibility of the Pope is hedged about by so many restrictions that it amounts to very little. If we admit that two recent popes have done more to advance the cause of Christian charity than all of the scattered efforts of a divided Protestantism in a hundred years, it is easy to see the opportunities for concerted action of all Christendom in an undivided church.

Some years ago, during a two-man Protestant-Catholic dialogue which ran non-stop for four years, my Catholic friend suggested to me the possibility of union by a very simple formula. "It would be easy," he said, with what I thought was fantastic optimism. "Just suppose that the Protestants who hold to the great doctrines of the Christian Faith, yet who differ from each other and the Roman Catholics in matters of ritual, ceremony, and administration, should wish to unite. If they were to seek to unite Roman Catholics and Protestants in a really Catholic Church, all they would have to do, in fact, would be to accept the Pope as the head of the Church and come right in."

Frankly, I was completely incredulous. I asked, "What about all these differences in our ways of worship?"

And then he pointed out that there were perfectly good Roman Catholics who did not use the Latin in saying Mass, who permitted their clergy to marry, whose liturgy differed greatly from the Roman liturgy; yet they were in the Church.

I thought the matter over for a while, and then I said, "It sounds wonderful, but there is one catch to it. At the present time, there is not a chance that any Protestant group would ever accept the Pope as the supreme leader of the Church."

But that was twenty years ago, and times (and Popes) have changed since then. Protestants now have a vastly better understanding of the Catholic Church than we had in those days. We have become used to church organizations which are, in some cases, just as centralized in authority as the Roman Church. Those non-Catholic Christians who have lived under the leadership of the Archbishop of Canterbury and thrived, might not find it hard to look to Rome for fatherly advice and instruction. Methodists who have flourished under the most autocratic system of episcopal supervision ever invented, would find, perhaps, even less interference with their independence than they now happily accept.

Two stumbling blocks stand across the road to union. One is the dogma of Papal infallibility, the other the Assumption of the Virgin Mary. Both doctrines are extrabiblical, finding their justification in tradition, rather than in the Bible. It would seem to the outsider that the leaders of the Roman Catholic Church have in these two instances bowed to the wishes of the common people and accepted a "lowest common denominator" of popular piety. It is true that the dogma of infallibility is popular with the faithful and had been accepted many hundreds of years before it was promulgated. As I have mentioned in the previous chapter, this teaching, when properly understood is unobjectionable to many Protestants who can accept the explanation that infallibility extends only into the field of doctrine, as established by the Church. To some extent this may be similar to a recognized leader of a denomination interpreting the doctrines of his group. It is true, however, that few Roman Catholics understand it in this fashion and almost all Protestants see it as fantastic exaggeration of the mental and spiritual powers of a man who has been elected head of the Church.

No one can deny that both Pope John XXIII and Pope Paul VI seem to understand their infallibility as dealing entirely with matters of doctrine and interpretation. Pope Paul, in an address to the Second Vatican Council, said,

> In a sense, we recognize in ourself the figure of a humble worshiper, our Predecessor Honorius II. He is portrayed adoring Christ in a beautiful mosaic in the apse of the Basilica of St. Paul. That Pontiff of short stature is represented there prostrate, kissing the feet of a Christ of gigantic dimensions. This Christ, in the likeness of a royal and majestic teacher, presides over and blesses the people gathered in the Basilica—a symbol of the Church.[11]

A significant address to the 1963 session of the Council was made by Archbishop Joseph Descuffi of Smyrna who offered an interpretation of the dogma of infallibility which would go far toward brushing away some of the misunderstanding. He argued that there were two infallibilities involved, that of the Pope and that of the Church, and pointed out that the definition given by Council Father Gasser at the First Vatican Council leaves room for both Church and Pontiff as sources of truth. He quotes Fr. Gasser as saying:

> Another reason why we do not exclude the cooperation of the Church is that the infallibility of the Roman Pontiff is not something which comes to him by inspiration or revelation but by the help of God. It follows from this that the Pope, because of his responsibility and the seriousness of the matter, is bound to use appropriate means to search out and suitably express the truth: such means are councils or even the advice of bishops, cardinals, theologians, etc.[12]

---

[11] Hans Kung, Yves Congar, and Daniel O'Hanlon, eds., *Council Speeches of Vatican II* (Glen Rock, N.J.: Paulist Press, 1964), p. 21.

[12] Ibid., pp. 68-69.

In other words, the infallibility of the Pope is seen in his right to express the mind of the Church, presupposing the guidance of the Holy Spirit. It has nothing to do with the popular interpretation that the Holy Father never makes a mistake or commits a sin—a notion which is entirely false. He must confess his sins the same as any priest; he can make mistakes in any of the ways open to very fallible men. But when he speaks with the backing of the Church, having been taught through scripture and tradition, concerning matters of faith, he is to be heard by the faithful. Speaking *ex cathedra,* as Supreme Pontiff and teacher of the Church, having consulted the Church through the Councils or other groups in the Church, he is speaking for the Church.

But, says Fr. Gasser, "The Pope alone does not constitute the Church; but where the Pope is, there is the true Church in agreement with him."[13]

Soon after the promulgation of the dogma of the Assumption of the Blessed Virgin, I visited a Roman Catholic friend and, in the course of the conversation, expressed my disappointment that the Pope would choose the time when Catholic and Protestant relations were growing more cordial to issue such a statement. "It will set us back twenty years," I said. "Protestants cannot understand why it should be necessary to add to our confusion and give the Catholics one more 'impossible thing to believe before breakfast,' in the manner of the Red Queen."

My friend smiled. "Cheer up," he said, "and just be glad that *you* don't have to accept it!" That was his only comment. I gathered that he might have some reservations in his own mind. But another priest commented, "It seems to be the policy of the Church that when Catholics seem to be getting a little relaxed she gives them something hard to chew on. Perhaps there is a fear that the faithful may get spiritually lazy unless they have to work hard at believing something out of the ordinary."

This was more than a decade ago, and now we hear very little about the Assumption, although I realize that this statement regarding the Virgin Mother has been current in the Church for

---

[13] Op. cit., pp. 70-71.

many centuries, and seems to be perfectly acceptable to the rank and file of the laity. But the consensus of untutored opinion often leads us astray, and to make official dogma which finds no support in Scripture simply because it is popular among the common people may be dangerous. This alone would hinder my own acceptance of any exaggerated idea of papal infallibility; surely this must have been one time when a slight mistake crept in!

Yet we must recognize that there has been a vast change in the Catholic Church in the last few years, and this change has been shown in the down-grading of many of the former emphases upon the Saints and the Virgin Mary. The Mother of Christ still holds a high place in the teaching of the Catholic Church, and justly so, but the present emphasis is upon her place as a part of the Church.

There are many problems to be faced in the march toward unity —problems that may today seem to be insurmountable. Some of the most difficult, on the surface, may be overcome by understanding, for it is certainly true that we do not yet understand each other, and that we fear, instead of trust, each other. In conversations with Protestant ministers, of my own and other denominations, I have learned that there is still a great gulf fixed between Protestants and Catholics, a gulf of misunderstanding based on ignorance.

The road to unity is long and difficult, but there has been more progress in the last four years than in the past four hundred. Further progress depends upon two things: (1) the attitude of the Roman Catholic leaders, (2) the willingness of Protestants to put aside preconceived ideas regarding the Catholic Church and to accept the fact of the new Catholic reformation.

But the possibility of much greater cooperation between the two great groups of Western Christians can be brought much closer by the current liturgical revival among Protestants and Catholics. It is to this new mood of interest in common worship that we turn next.

Chapter Six

Liturgy and Christian Unity

Two areas of study have been particularly effective in bringing together Roman Catholic and Protestant scholars. During the past fifteen years unprecedented cooperation in biblical and liturgical research has brought together experts in these fields from both sides of the "fence." Roman Catholic scholars have made notable strides in this field, but have freely acknowledged their debt to their Protestant brethren.

In the field of liturgical studies, the situation has been reversed, with Protestant scholars looking to Roman Catholics for guidance, especially in the study of worship in the Church prior to the Reformation. Although they find much to question in the writings of such authorities as Adrian Fortescue, F. Cabrol, Cardinal Bellarmin, L. Duchesne, and others, they have found in these books a breadth of liturgical knowledge unmatched among Protestants until recent times.

As would be expected, Anglicans have contributed much to Liturgical study, and the monumental book by Dom Gregory Dix, *The Shape of the Liturgy* (London: Adam and Charles Black, Ltd., 1945), was instrumental in encouraging many Protestant students to begin a serious examination of worship. During the last fifteen years many excellent volumes on the subject have been written by Lutheran, Episcopal, Reformed, and Presbyterian scholars.

It is in this field that Protestants (and Anglicans) have found common ground of interest and fellowship. Recently a group of twelve unofficial representatives of Protestant denominations and the Catholic Church met to discuss liturgical problems and found, to their surprise, that they were almost of one mind on all subjects touched upon at the meeting. It is true that there were many points of theology upon which they would not have agreed, but there was no controversy over the liturgy.

Points of Agreement

Protestants and Catholics can agree that the worship of God is the prime work of the Church, and they very generally agree with Dix when he says:

> "Liturgy" is the name given ever since the days of the apostles to the act of taking part in the corporate worship of God by the "priestly" society of Christians, who are "the Body of Christ, the Church." "The Liturgy" is the term which covers generally all that worship which is officially organized by the Church, and which is open to and offered by, or in the name of, all who are members of the Church. It distinguishes this from the personal prayers of the individual Christians who make up the Church, and even from the common prayer of selected or voluntary groups within the Church, e.g., guilds or societies. In the course of time the term "The Liturgy" has come to be particularly applied to the performance of that rite which was instituted by our Lord Jesus Christ Himself to be the peculiar and distinctive worship

> of those who should be "His Own," and which has ever been the heart and core of Christian worship and Christian living—the Eucharist or Breaking of Bread.[1]

Dix makes one further statement which is the basis for general agreement among liturgical scholars:

> In the later fourth century, when our knowledge is more definite, we find three facts which can be taken as certain: (*a*) The outline of the rite—the Shape of the Liturgy—is everywhere most remarkably the same, after 300 years of independent existence in the widely scattered churches. (*b*) The content of the eucharistic prayer is by then also to some extent the same in arrangement and even in certain phrases. But (*c*) the great historic families show strongly marked peculiarities of their own.[2]

Today we deal with the results of some of these peculiarities and others, which are the product of the long years of liturgical neglect and the prevalence of innovations for the sake of change. Protestants and Catholics are alike chargeable with this fault. Among Catholics, as we have seen, the excesses of the Middle Ages produced confusion in the Liturgy, as various rites were merged without due care to see that they did not conflict, and, among Protestants, the independence of the reforming groups and their tendency to de-emphasize the Eucharist in favor of variations upon the form of Morning Prayer contributed to the general confusion regarding the purpose and meaning of worship.

Roman Catholic Worship Prior to Vatican II

Michael J. Taylor describes some of the ways in which Catholic worship deteriorated during the centuries. The Protestant observer, looking on from the outside, may notice some things that are not apparent to those within the Church. This is true because, perhaps, his view is less likely to be colored by the rosy glow of child-

---

[1] Gregory Dix, *The Shape of the Liturgy* (London: A. & C. Black, Ltd., 1945), p. 1.
[2] Op. cit., p. 5.

hood memories and the warm hue of faith. Things which to the non-Catholic appear to be useless and even a hindrance to worship, may, when looked upon as a part of a great tradition, seem excusable as ministering to the popular piety of the uneducated.

One of the most commonly criticized elements in the Roman Mass is the position of the priest, who has for centuries, stood with his back to the people, with his body hiding the movements of his hands, except for the high moment when he bows over the Bread and cries, *"Hoc est enim corpus meum."* Protestants have spent a great deal of time and energy arguing that this "priestly" attitude of the celebrant is contrary to the New Testament idea of Christ, despite the fact that few of them have ever witnessed the Mass. We have repeated the old objections over and over, until, at last, Catholics have, themselves, accepted them and changed the position back to the ancient one. Somehow, I doubt whether Protestant objections are responsible for the change, for I am quite sure that it is the study of customs of the ancient church that has brought this about. Nevertheless, it is good to see that one barrier to understanding has been removed. The position of the priest may not have violated any theological doctrines, but it most certainly encouraged inattention on the part of the congregation!

The use of Latin in the Mass has also contributed to the lack of appreciation by Protestants, and, I think, Catholics, as well. Father Taylor has, in following chapters, disposed of this matter in excellent fashion. The Liturgical Renewal in the Catholic Church seeks to make the Mass understood by the people, which is exactly what Cranmer hoped to do, and did, in his *Book of Common Prayer*. Despite the fact that the sonorous and beautiful Latin becomes, after a while, a part of the attraction of the Mass, even to non-Catholics, it does not make the Mass intelligible to the congregation.

Yet there are pitfalls lurking for the unwary in the new use of the vernacular. As one Protestant lecturer ventured to suggest to a group of priests, it is much easier to run through the Mass in Latin than it will be to read or sing it in English so that the people can understand. Even Protestant ministers have been known to mumble the Communion service!

Congregational Participation

Lack of participation in worship is a fault not confined to Catholics, for the Reformed congregations soon fell into the habit (a hold-over from medieval practice) of sitting in silence while the minister conducted the service from the pulpit. As time went on, and the celebration of Holy Communion became more and more infrequent, sermons became longer and longer, and little was left to the people to do.

But for hundreds of years Catholics have been accustomed to a measure of inactivity unknown in the ancient Church. Where once they had joined in almost all parts of the Mass, through hymns and responses and prayers, they, at length, lapsed into a passivity broken only by gestures of genuflecting, kneeling, standing, and making the sign of the cross. None of these is in any sense objectionable, and could well be carried over into non-Catholic worship, but they are not enough.

The Reformation, under Luther, brought back the ancient custom of singing, and this, perhaps, had more to do with the success of the movement than anything else. Not only did Luther introduce the hymn into all of the services, he wrote hymns in the language of the people and set them to tunes that were popular and singable. Many years later, Wesley followed his lead, and Methodism was borne on wings of song throughout the world. It is to these hymns popularized by the Methodist revival that Protestantism owes its comparative uniformity of worship patterns, and, more than that, its practical agreement in theology, for whatever differences there were between the followers of Calvin, Luther, and Knox, they were, in time, almost forgotten as their disciples sang songs of salvation. The Arminian theology of Wesley, in violent opposition to Calvinism, could not withstand the fervent piety of Watts and Toplady and, on the other hand, Calvinists soon learned to sing with enthusiasm Charles Wesley's "Jesus, Lover of My Soul."

The Catholic Church, which gave the world such masterpieces of Christian hymns as, "Te Deum Laudamus," "O Splendor of

God's Glory Bright," and, much later, "Faith of Our Fathers," is now returning to the practice of singing hymns, and this development may result in the production of a hymnbook which will be made up of selections from both Catholic and Protestant sources. Such a book is already in preparation, for use in ecumenical gatherings.

But at present the average congregation at Mass is somewhat bewildered by the new ways of worship and wary of change. To be told that they must sing, say responses, and read prayers, instead of sitting quietly, may seem completely foreign to Catholic worship, but it is the pattern of the future.

A recent news story in a Catholic newspaper quoted a priest as urging Catholics to learn to sing like Protestants, and calling upon composers to write more simple melodies for the congregations to sing at divine services. He criticized Catholic composers for writing difficult masterpieces instead of songs that the people could sing, and he reminded his hearers that early Church music was simple, and sung by the entire congregation.

Changes in the Liturgy

The second session of the Second Vatican Council produced few concrete proposals, but one of these will have far-reaching consequences. The promulgation of the Constitution on the Liturgy set in motion a long-time program of reform in the worship of the Church. These may be summarized as follows:

1. The official use of the vernacular in the Scripture readings and the parts of the Mass which are properly said or sung by the people.
2. A new lectionary giving greater variety and better selections in the Epistles and Gospels.
3. Sermons to be required as an integral part of the Mass.
4. A "people's prayer" to be restored and inserted after the Gospel and homily, to ask God's blessing on the Church, diocese, and parish, for those in need and for all mankind.

One of the most interesting developments (at least to Protestants) was the Council's decision to allow the Communion under both species on special occasions. These occasions are listed as being three: "to the newly ordained in the Mass of their sacred ordination, to the newly professed in the Mass of their religious profession, and to the newly baptized in the Mass which follows their Baptism." Frederick R. McManus, a member of the Post-Conciliar Commission on the Liturgy, explains:

> Communion in both kinds is not some privilege of the priests, and thus one example is given for the clergy (including deacons and subdeacons and even the lesser orders), the religious and the laity. Already the hope among the laity, certainly in countries where the level of religious education is high, is that the practice will be extended to the wedding Mass, to the occasions of first Communion, and Confirmation, and the like."[3]

Fr. McManus reminds us that this development, while not entirely satisfactory to some, at least "shows the willingness of the Church to attempt a renewal." "It should," he says, "overcome, as no apologetic explanation would ever do, the charge that the laity are denied the cup of the Lord's Blood. It shows respect for the usage of the Eastern Churches, both Orthodox and Catholic."

Even more significant, to Protestants, is his explanation behind the restoration. "What," he asks, "is the purpose of restoring Communion under both kinds? The answer lies in the nature of the Eucharist as food and drink, as a holy meal. The Eucharistic sacrifice or Mass was instituted by Christ in the form of a family meal, a banquet of the community which is the Church. Any experience, any sign, any outward evidence that we eat the Lord's Flesh and drink His Blood makes our participation a holier thing."

And he continues:

> In modern times no Catholic has doubted that the Mass is a true sacrifice offered to God; that is beyond question. *That it is a sacred meal of food and drink has not penetrated very deeply into Catholic consciousness at times* [italics ours]. It is not enough for the Council to decree: "Efforts must also be made to encourage a sense of community within the parish, above all in the common celebration of Sunday Mass." The Council must also

[3] Frederick R. McManus, *Our Sunday Visitor,* June 21, 1964.

put this into effect by restoring the fullness of understanding of the Mass.[4]

Protestants will see in the proposal, limited as it is, the vindication of Luther's insistence on the restoration of the Cup to the congregation. If this be carried further, the Protestant objection that the laity do not really *commune* in the traditional manner will be done away. Actually, the denial of the Cup was never a matter of doctrine, but simply a regulation adopted in a time when abuses were common and when the fear of sacrilege overrode all other considerations. The danger that a drop of the precious Blood would be spilled loomed large in the minds of the leaders of the Church, and thus the tradition of the early days was broken in an effort to protect the sacred ceremony.

If Communion in both kinds is generally adopted, one of the minor barriers between Protestants and Catholics will have been hurdled.

Another reform coming from the Council has little bearing upon Protestant-Catholic relations, but is significant in that it shows a tendency to change old customs and to adjust to the tempo of the times. For hundreds of years, Catholic priests have felt that they should say Mass each day, even though there were no communicants or congregation. This has seemed to make the Mass, or Holy Communion, instead of a family meal, a private exercise of the priest, an obligation to be fulfilled, often at the cost of great inconvenience. The latter is, of course, no argument, for the devoted priest or minister must be willing to endure hardship, but in these days of many meetings of priests together, it seems unnecessary to require that each one find an unoccupied altar for his private Mass, when the Mass is being celebrated in a public service. The new ruling makes it possible for priests to "concelebrate," that is, fulfill their duty and privilege by offering the Eucharist together with their brethren and the assembled congregation. Thus the spectacle of many side altars in a large church or monastery may, in time, be out of date, and on such occasions as the great Liturgical Week, attended by thousands of priests, it will be possible for

[4] Op. cit.

them to join together in the Eucharist, instead of scattering all over the city in search of altars for their private Masses.

Fr. McManus has this to say about concelebration:

> It shows the meaning of the holy order of priesthood—a college, a body, a community into which men are ordained to be collaborators and cooperators of the bishop, and the servants or ministers of the people.
>
> Even though it has not yet issued its constitution "on the Church," the Second Vatican Council has already proclaimed the nature of the Church as an assembly of worshipers. Communion under both kinds, concelebration and the whole revision of the rite of holy Mass will gradually make this doctrine concrete, a matter of Sunday practice in the parish which is the Church in miniature.[5]

It is this growing realization of the Church "as the praying people of God" that will give a firm basis for conversations on unity between Catholics and non-Catholics, and will, in time, God willing, bring us closer to each other.

The Hope of Unity

In the first flush of ecumenical enthusiasm, Protestants and Catholics were tempted to speak in optimistic tones concerning the possibility of church union. Mistaking the dawn of an awakening sympathy and love for the full glow of noonday, they looked forward to speedy unification. Of course, only a few went this far, and they were cancelled out by the die-hard conservatives in both camps who branded such optimistic thoughts as fantastic. The majority took a middle path and counseled moderation in speech and a check-rein on imagination. Union of the many Protestant denominations had not come, nor was it even possible, they said, and certainly union of such divergent ways of worship and doctrine would take many years—perhaps centuries. All we could hope for at this time was an increased sympathy and understanding.

The conservatives have been proved wrong by the events of the

[5] Frederick R. McManus, op. cit.

last three years; it remains to be seen whether the optimism of the proponents of speedy unification of Protestants and Catholics are right in their supposition that now is the time for a miracle. But certainly no one could have foreseen the remarkable advance on the road to unity since the beginning of Vatican II.

Those who have kept up with ecumenical developments on a day-to-day basis by reading the newspapers and the religious journals may be excused for a bit of optimism regarding the long-term hope for a merger of leading Protestant groups with the Roman Catholic Church. Barriers are falling like bricks from a bull-dozed wall; old misconceptions are being brushed away from our windows of denominational outlook; daring schemes are being proposed which, a few years ago, would have provoked scornful laughter.

For example: A news story in a prominent Catholic weekly tells of a speech by a Roman Catholic priest and teacher who suggests that the Catholic Youth Organization should speedily merge with the Young Men's Christian Association! Remembering that, a few years ago, Catholic youth were forbidden by some bishops to attend the Y.M.C.A., I am wondering if the next step will be a proposal to unite the Knights of Columbus and the Masonic Lodge! (But, as I write this, comes news that a proposal has already been made that these two organizations cooperate in good works!)

But why not join forces? Perhaps such a merger as that of the two great youth organizations could be arranged; certainly it would be advantageous in every way, and, as both are Christian groups with similar aims, yet not too closely tied to denominational positions on theology, the plan might work. The speaker might have been sending up a trial balloon, but he may have started something.

In the same issue appeared a story concerning a speech by a Dutch theologian which suggested the possibility that "the office of pope would be limited to a specific tenure instead of being for life." [6] Father F. Haarsma, theological adviser of the Dutch hierarchy for the Second Vatican Council is quoted as saying that the essential Catholic concept of Christian reunion—"the return to the one Church under the one Pontiff"—did not rule out the

---

[6] F. Haarsma, *Our Sunday Visitor,* June 28, 1964.

possibility of major changes in the office of the Papacy, and asked, "Can we say at this moment how far those changes will lead the Church? . . . The Catholic conviction is that the Church without Peter and the other apostles is unthinkable. But this does not preclude the fact that, with the common reflection of all Christians on the Bible and tradition, under the Holy Spirit, the pontifical office might take on a form which we cannot now possibly foresee." [7]

Whether or not there will ever be a change such as this, the implication of these words are important, for they indicate a willingness to reconsider and re-evaluate old positions—something that Protestants have supposed was impossible under the Roman system.

On the Protestant side there have been many indications of a new attitude of friendliness and understanding toward the Roman Catholic Church. These incidents of goodwill have not been well publicized and it is possible that they have not been as numerous. There is a reason for this. Protestantism is not united; it has no central headquarters and no one who can speak for all its various groups.

The denominations which have tacitly, and sometimes actively, supported the ecumenical movement find it difficult to adjust to the widening interpretation of the word "ecumenism." For years they have thought in terms of Protestant unity (itself yet an unfulfilled dream) and the prospect of dealing with the hope of a united Christendom has often seemed too difficult. "If we can't unite all the Lutherans, all the Methodists, and all the Presbyterians and Baptists, how can we expect to get together with the Roman Catholics?" is the question on the lips of the majority of Protestants.

I confess that I, too, am staggered by the task. Yet what we see as almost impossible seems not quite so formidable to our Catholic friends, for they are used to dealing with large groups through powerful leaders. It is hard for them to understand, for instance, that The Methodist Church in America has no "head" in the sense of a supreme bishop; it is ruled by a General Conference, composed of representatives from all over the world. Legislation is

---

[7] Ibid.

proposed by committees and often dictated by the various special interests concerned. So far, there is no Commission on Protestant-Catholic Unity, although there is a commission for Ecumenical affairs which may expand its field during the next four years.

The Methodist predicament is shared by other denominations, for each must work in similar fashion. Thus any great ecumenical effort, must, in effect, come from the grass roots and overwhelm the leadership, who are of necessity so immersed in the usual duties of keeping the machinery of the organization oiled and working that they have little time for extra activities. It is, however, encouraging to note that bishops and presiding officers of various titles in the denominations are showing great interest in the new movement toward brotherhood. Their acceptance or rejection of the unity movement will not be the final test, however. That depends upon the pastors and the laity, the majority of whom are not yet actively interested, nor very well informed.

First Steps to Unity

If organic union must be considered as belonging only to the distant future (as I believe it must be), what then can we do to further the cause of unity in Catholic and Protestant worship? The distinction between unity and union may be a bit of hairsplitting, but it can serve to clarify the situation.

Union of Christendom presupposes, at least, according to the Roman Catholic idea, one Church, with one head, the Pope; with one general type of ecclesiastical organization; one body of doctrine; one aim, and one faith in Christ as the Son of God.

Unity, on the other hand, can be defined, for our purpose, at least, as an attitude. When Catholics and Protestants seek the same goal—the Christianization of the world; when they tacitly, or officially, agree on the general purpose and the means to the end; when they find themselves bound to each other in a fellowship of believers by cords of Christian love; when they can worship together in prayer and praise, cooperate in works of charity; unite in efforts to further the common good—when they do these things they will have achieved a measure of unity.

This is, I admit, unity in its lowest form, but it is a unity which was blessed in the early Church. The theory that all Christians of the first two centuries were under the one ecclesiastical head seems untenable in the light of present knowledge. Church machinery did not extend that far. We may acknowledge that the Bishop of Rome was very early accepted as the titular head of the Church, yet there was no uniform exercise of authority such as came to be in the years that followed. Perhaps today we have more spiritual leadership from Rome than was ever the case in the first three centuries, for, through the medium of modern communications, non-Catholic Christians have been able to hear the Pope speak, to learn to admire him as a man and follow him as a leader. But many of those who gladly accept him as a great religious authority and a spiritual guide are not willing to admit that he should have *supreme* power, even over the Roman Catholic Church. In that Church there are many who argue against giving to the Pope such powers as were assumed in the Middle Ages, and, from all indications, modern popes are unwilling to demand the unlimited authority which was once their acknowledged due.

Union of all Christendom is to be desired and hoped for, but it is not a *necessity*. God *has* long worked through a divided Church. The Holy Spirit *can* speak to men of differing opinions and can lead through various channels.

Let us look at some suggested steps to Christian unity.

1. *We can be united in faith in Jesus Christ as the Son of God, our Savior*. This unity of faith is already present, for all Christians who hold to the doctrinal standards of the traditional church groups hold this proposition to be central.

But such a belief must work out in practice. If we Protestants agree that we hold this faith in company with our Roman Catholic brethren, then we must proceed upon that assumption. We must not impute to them doctrines which they do not believe; we must not exaggerate our criticism of certain differences in practice, such as the veneration of saints, the fervent love for the Mother of Christ, the little pious acts of devotion which are not practiced among us. Instead we must try to understand how these differences originated in past years and in very different surroundings. In the words of the popular saying, "We must accentuate the positive." We must look for the points of agreement and consider whether or not they outweigh the disagreements.

2. *We can be united in action.* At a time when Christianity is facing the first major attack from other religions since the rise of the Muslim faith we must prepare to meet the challenge of non-Christian religions. Buddhism, Islam, and paganism confront us on all sides. Our response must be united, as our faith must be firm. We must not fight with material weapons, but with love and compassion, seeking to know the good that is in other faiths, but offering the "much more" that is in Jesus Christ.

Here at home the forces of a pagan civilization threaten to overturn our Christian concepts of home and community life. Can we afford to be divided at a time like this? Can we afford to argue over small matters while our house is burning down?

To be specific, Catholic priests and Protestant ministers must cooperate in organizations for mutual help and encouragement. This is already taking place, as priests and ministers join together in religious and social activities in many communities where such cooperation was unknown a few years ago. The outcome is certain: We will learn to love each other as we learn to understand each other.

3. *But if we are to really understand, we must pray together.* Oddly enough, this is one of the most difficult steps in the march toward unity. Protestants have long been considered by Roman Catholics as "not-quite" Christian, and Roman Catholics have been targets for virulent criticism by Protestants. Only a few years have elapsed since ministers and priests were afraid of being seen together on the streets, much less visiting each other. We have not yet found a way to worship together in our churches, except by the use of new forms of nonliturgical services; yet we have made so much progress that we are asking why we cannot go further.

True, we can and do pray *for* each other, and recently it has been possible to join in saying the Lord's Prayer together in special services. This is done with the approval of Roman Catholic authorities and with the encouragement of the Pope. But this is not enough. Protestants may, and do, visit Catholic Churches and take part in the Mass, but cannot receive Holy Communion. They are now considered spiritual members of the Catholic Church, by baptism, but full communion awaits clarification of the basis of such communion.

Asked why Protestant observers at a recent Liturgical Week could not commune, one priest suggested that it was because they had not gone to confession. Another prominent Catholic clergyman went much further and gave his opinion that, if the Protestant were not in a state of mortal sin, confession would not be required, and he would be justified in approaching the Lord's Table. The question for Catholics is, however, whether such action would not give rise to "scandal" by weakening the authority of the Church. An authoritative pronouncement from the Vatican would clarify the situation, and such might be forthcoming.

Among Protestants, there is no complete agreement on the qualifications necessary for participating in the Communion. Episcopalians, in their Ritual, invite those who "truly and earnestly repent of (their) sins and are in love and charity with (their) neighbors, and intend to lead a new life, following the commandments of God, and walking from henceforth in his holy ways. . . ."

Methodists have almost the same words, as do some other denominations. Yet, in some cases, Episcopalian priests have denied Communion to Methodists and others, on the grounds that they have not been confirmed by an Episcopalian bishop. Thus Protestants, as well as Catholics, need to study the basis for participation in the Sacrament of Holy Communion.

As there is no public service in the Catholic Church similar to that of Morning Prayer (although, of course, this roughly corresponds to the monastic Matins), Protestants, who might easily join with their Catholic brethren in such a service, must be content to attend Mass without receiving Communion. We may assume that no Protestant would be disciplined in any way for attending a Catholic service, but the same does not apply to a Catholic who might wish to attend a Protestant worship service. Will there be further relaxation of regulations to permit this? There are indications that there will be, for, already, priests are being granted permission to do so, on certain occasions.

The reason for the disinclination of Catholic authorities to permit lay participation or visitation in Protestant Churches is logical, in view of past history, for, until recently, the Catholic might have been embarrassed by criticism of the Catholic Church. This is now almost a thing of the past, and it would seem that there might be further progress along this line in the coming years.

There is, however, a way in which we can pray together, if not in the Mass or the service of Holy Communion. There are now occasions when Protestant ministers and Catholic priests join together in discussions and in prayer under various forms. We can always say the Lord's Prayer together, and there are other prayers which are a part of the common heritage of the historic church. And, until further clarification of the matter is received from the Vatican, it may not be possible to go further than this.

Protestants generally recognize that the difficulty is not found in an attitude of superiority on the part of the Catholic Church, but it is rooted in something much deeper, the fear of making *invalid* the celebration of the Mass. This question of validity is discussed at length by Fr. Adrian Nocent, in a recent volume, *The Future of the Liturgy*. The author voices the feeling of many modern Catholics that too much emphasis has been placed upon the mechanical:

> In all times and in all religions there has always appeared a mass tendency toward an easy sort of divine mechanism set in action by a rite. To make religion into a kind of convenient servitude to ritual practices carried out like beneficent magic has always been and will always be the dream of mankind, who would like to secure the favors of the divinity at the lowest price, without surrendering the depths of themselves. . . . The Council (of Trent) cannot be blamed for the stiffened and warped orientation of theologians of the Counter-Reformation in the direction of "validism." [8]

It is this fear of invalidation which causes Catholics to draw back from any participation in regular Protestant religious services, especially Holy Communion, and to deny the right of Protestants to receive Communion in a Catholic Church. There are indications that this barrier may be surmounted in the coming years.

The way to unity is being made plainer as Protestants and Roman

[8] Adrian Nocent, *The Future of the Liturgy* (New York: Herder & Herder, Inc., 1964), pp. 23-24.

Catholics attempt to formulate a basis of ecumenical understanding. This goes deeper than mere speculation upon the future; it is based upon a study of the nature of the Church and the relation of Protestant denominations to the Church. Catholic scholars interested in liturgy and unity are now engaged upon such a study and a small bimonthly magazine, called *The Ecumenist* is leading the way. In a recent issue, the editor, Fr. Gregory Baum, discusses the question, "What Are Other Churches?" and suggests that Catholics should not refuse to consider non-Catholic communities as "Churches," despite the fact that, organically, they are separated from what Catholics believe to be the true Church.

"Is there," he asks, "a theological foundation, and not only a sociological or phenomenological one, for regarding Anglican and Protestant communities as ecclesiastical realities?"

Fr. Baum acknowledges that there are difficulties in the way of complete acceptance of the catholicity of these groups, but he goes on to say:

> At the same time, we must be willing to acknowledge that these separated Christians proclaim the Kingdom of God. They preach the Gospel, they celebrate holy baptism, and they declare the Eucharistic signs in the midst of their congregations. There can be no doubt that they are instruments—in various degrees, defective instruments—through which God saves and sanctifies those whom he has chosen. And if God deigns to give grace through and in these Communions and to accept the worship offered by them, then the Catholic people ought not to acknowledge this grudgingly, by way of concession, but with joy and gratitude, confident that this divine action, far from harming, will help the spiritual growth of the Church.
>
> It is important for us to reflect on the supernatural character of dissident Christian Communion, since this will give us the right understanding of ecumenism. The ecumenical movement is not concerned with individuals; it does not consist in proclaiming the special self-awareness of the Church to other Christians to attract them to us. Ecumenism is not a subtle form of convert-making. A Christian who discovers the Catholic Church to be the place where the promises of God are being fulfilled must follow his conscience and join her, but to persuade others of this is not the aim of ecumenism.
>
> The ecumenical movement deals not with individuals, but

> with Communions. It is a movement for unity engaging the Church and the Communions separated from her in dialogue, seeking mutual understanding, finding wider areas of cooperation, and by discussion and research striving for greater balance in the possession of the Gospel. Ecumenism opens the Churches to the action of the Spirit, drawing them into greater fidelity to Christ. In this way the Churches converge as they are being renewed. Ecumenism is not, in the first place, a matter of ecclesiastical negotiation. It is a movement of evangelical renewal, and as the Churches grow in the likeness of Christ they shall advance on the road to unity.[9]

Cooperation in the Study of the Liturgy

One of the most encouraging signs of the new day is seen in the founding of the World Center for Liturgical Studies, a cooperative venture by Protestant, Anglican, Orthodox, and Roman Catholic scholars. Started by an Episcopalian priest, Canon Don A. Copeland of Boca Raton, Fla., the organization is composed of representatives from the various groups all over the world. One goal of the organization is the establishment of a World Center at Boca Raton, where scholars can come for a period of residence and study at a library which, it is hoped, will contain microfilmed copies of the liturgical treasures of the churches. Seminars would be held during the year and special studies initiated. One proposed project is that of a common hymnbook which could be used in ecumenical gatherings by Protestants, Orthodox, and Roman Catholics. The Center idea has received enthusiastic support from the leading liturgists of the various communions.

Protestant and Anglican liturgical scholars are now engaged in a continuing dialogue through the medium of various magazines whose columns are open to writers from both sides of the fast-vanishing fence. An Episcopalian scholar, Dr. Massey H. Shepherd, is an associate editor of the Catholic *Yearbook of Liturgical Studies,* edited by Fr. John H. Miller (Fides Publishers, Notre Dame, Ind.), and Protestants are frequent contributors to other Catholic magazines.

---

[9] Gregory Baum, *The Ecumenist* (New York: Paulist Press, Nov.-Dec. 1963).

Many American Catholic dioceses have appointed directors of ecumenical work who are receiving hearty cooperation from Protestant ministerial associations in their efforts to promote understanding, not by minimizing problems but by meeting them frankly. Such efforts are bearing fruit in better understanding and often agreement upon problems which were once thought to be insoluble.

Signs of Progress

As we come to the close of this discussion, the third session of Vatican Council II is in progress. Contrary to the predictions of some, there has been no letdown in interest or in progress toward ecumenicity. Some non-Catholic commentators have interpreted the words of Pope Paul VI, in a recent statement, as an indication that he would be less likely to encourage further steps toward ecumenical action. This, I believe, is a mistaken opinion, based upon a reading of what the Holy Father did not say. We must realize that the new attitude of the Pope toward the bishops—an attitude which reverses the trend toward absolutism and emphasizes the collegiality of the bishops and their authority to make decisions "on their own," must of necessity preclude any far-reaching and radical pronouncements from the Vatican.

Already, the log-jam accumulated through the centuries has been broken, and it seems likely that nothing can stop the rushing flood of *aggiornamento,* or updating, of the Church. This reformation is in progress now, and will continue. It is probable that the next few years will see many changes made in ceremonies, ritual, and attitudes toward other Christians. Indeed, the changes already permitted are astounding to those who know the Roman Catholic Church only as a monolithic organization, wedded to ancient ways and impervious to the winds of change.

Protestants must study these changes in order to understand what is taking place. As a matter of fact, many of the objections mentioned in these chapters are no longer valid, except as reminders of what *has been* "official" and is now only customary. It will take time for these changes to filter down to the local congregations, and, in many places, it is possible that they will not come for many years, due to the opposition of some in authority and to the inevitable resistance to change which is inherent in any church organization.

Yet change is the order of the day. In the United States we may expect radical shifts in emphasis within the coming year. In Italy, for instance, it will take much longer. Here Catholics and Protestants are learning from each other; in many other countries there is no cross-fertilization of ideas, due to the fact that there are few Protestants. Mass in the vernacular is now officially prescribed in this country, yet there are Catholic congregations which will not accept it with enthusiasm, preferring to continue the old way of going to church to say their beads and secure a moment of quiet. Classes for instruction in the new ways are already being organized.

In August of 1964 the writer attended the annual Liturgical Week in St. Louis, Mo. With permission and full encouragement of Cardinal Ritter, Mass was celebrated in English for the first time in this country. Hymns were sung enthusiastically by the congregation of more than 15,000 Catholics and some one hundred Protestant guests, who were scattered through the auditorium without regard for church affiliation. These guests were able to take part in the Mass without difficulty and some of them realized, for the first time, that, stripped of much of its medieval trappings and said in English, the Mass was very similar to a Protestant service of Holy Communion.

But the most amazing change was seen in the use of Luther's great Reformation hymn, "A Mighty Fortress is Our God," at the processional hymn at the Mass celebrated by Cardinal Ritter.

Detained by an interview with a Catholic scholar, I was hurrying along the corridor, when suddenly I heard the vast audience singing. For a moment I did not realize what was happening, and when I did, I could hardly believe it, for these Catholics were singing, with fervor seldom heard in Protestant churches, the grand old hymn of the Reformation.

"Listen," I said to my Catholic friend. "Do I hear what I think I hear?"

And he smiled. "Indeed you do," he said, "and it's no accident, either. That hymn will be sung by us for many years, for it expresses the faith of a united Christian Church."

"Thank God," I said, "we're coming closer."

And so we are, for modern Catholics have found in Luther a symbol of reformation, a reformation which, this time, is going on within the Church. And in finding Luther, they are also finding their kinship with their Protestant brothers.

A CATHOLIC VIEWPOINT

Part One

Catholic Liturgy

Chapter One

The Idea of Catholic Liturgy

Liturgy, unity, the Church—to the Catholic these realities are inextricably bound up in the saving mystery of Christ. Christ has formed us from the many into the oneness of his Church. He has consecrated us a priestly people whose worship renders full praise to the Father as it unites us ever more deeply with him and with our brothers in the sanctifying oneness of his Body.

In our view there can be no doubt (allowing for the limitations of a Church built on men) what Christ wants his Church to be. His Incarnation brought us redemption and gave us a capacity for the perfect worship of the Father. It gave us a way to God; it offered us a share in the very truth and life of God himself. And with all the energies of his Incarnate life, Christ brought into being a Church whose acts of worship could render perfect praise to the Father; he set up a kingdom of grace where men could share in the way, the truth, and the life of God. This is the divine *koinonia,* as much of it as this earth will see until the *parousia.*

As prophetic preparation for the Christian Church, the Father had earlier formed the children of Abraham into a sacred people, a nation of priests, a worshiping community. In the desert under Moses' leadership, bound by covenant and law, he fashioned them into a religious assembly whose life of faith and ritual offered God a true and pleasing liturgy. Separate from other men, their worship, though only a prophetic shadow of the greater substance to come, was created pure in God's sight, a sign for all the nations to see and emulate.

And Christ, in fulfilling and perfecting the Father's covenant with Israel, did not change the nature of the chosen race as a worshiping, priestly people. He fashioned the believing remnant into a "new Israel," a visible kingdom of priests who would worship the Father in spirit and truth because they actually lived within the perfect priest, worshiper, and temple—Christ. God no longer signed his "chosen people" by circumcision, but sealed them in that sign of victory over death and glory in resurrection which is the miracle of Baptism. Their unity was no longer a matter of theocratic loyalties; it was a solidarity worked by the indwelling Spirit of Christ who formed all believers into a universal priesthood. Today the Church is even more God's nation of priests, his worshiping assembly.

The word *assembly* is about as close as we can come in English to the meaning of the biblical word which we translate as *church.* The Church of Jesus, then, is his assembly, a gathering of believers who discover in him a new, special relationship to the Father and to one another. It is a living union, as branches are joined to vine, as members of a body are one with their head. It is a personal union, as a bride is one with her groom in the unifying love-covenant of marriage. It is the union of temple stones whose aggregate rests upon the rock of Christ forming the perfect temple for the worship of the Father.

And the Christian enters this assembly as the ark of salvation, where, cleansed of his sins, he is able to worship God in full truth, to know and love him through grace. That grace brings newness of life, a new life in Christ. Man, since his first taste of divine indwelling, had always sought to live in God, but in his journey toward that life had completely lost his way. By himself he never found God. In fact, he had made himself an enemy through sin; by infidelity he brought on himself estrangement, exile and death. Clothed in sin and guilt he was incapable of happiness, unable to be what he knew he should be. He lived alone and with little hope.

But Jesus gave the answer to man's incapacity, confused searching, and guilt. In spite of our sins he became one of us, and as the Word made Flesh he undertook the human journey toward God himself so that sinful, misdirected man could follow him and be unburdened of sin and death and find a way to God. The pilgrim Christ became one of us and in his victory over sin and death gave us the means of forgiveness, the ability to know God and experience the highest form of unity, unity in the life of God himself. Our pilgrim Christ still lives, still forgives and directs us along the path to God and life; he lives and acts in his Church. And if men would seek salvation, they must enter into the Mystical Christ; they must love God in and with and through the Church, for the Church is Christ; it is his people, his royal priesthood, his consecrated nation.

Destined for membership in this priestly fellowship where he enters into the life and victory of Christ, the Christian is inserted into his Lord through the liturgy of Baptism. It is the rite of initiation, the liturgy of birth. This liturgy prepares for what we believe is the more perfect liturgy of the Mass, which edifies and nourishes the worshiping fellowship, increasing life in its members and creating an ever deeper solidarity between them and Christ. Baptism is a liturgy once-for-all. The Eucharist is the ongoing liturgy in which the Church regularly declares and realizes itself more fully in salvation and oneness. The Eucharist, or the Mass, is the Church's ritual worship of God. All other rites and sacraments are related and subordinate to it. Here the Catholic believes that he does what Christ commanded him to do "until he comes" (I Cor 11:26). Through the Mass the mystery of Christ is unfolded in Word and Sacrament; the saving acts of our Lord are celebrated and made present. In the Mass the faithful share in the reconciliation and the new life which God in the Flesh has purchased for us; the bonds of oneness with Christ and his Church are renewed and sealed.

Theoretically a Catholic could remove himself from parochial responsibilities and live a life detached from social action and missionary commitment and still be a minimal Christian. But if he refused to worship in the Church, to assist at Mass, in effect he would deny his faith. This is so because Catholics are primarily worshipers; they are secondarily missionaries. This is not to imply that a man could celebrate the Mass without some effect on his daily life, or that he could separate the liturgy completely from the effort to bring Christ to others through love and service. No one can pray the Mass properly without bringing to it and taking away a sense of commitment to love and serve the brothers. But there are many ways to love and serve. There is no substitute for the gathered assembly of Christ and its act of worship.

And a Christian does not gain admittance to this assembly of Christ because he is talented, moral, or intelligent. Jesus' parables make this clear. Wheat and weeds grow together in his kingdom, good fish swim with bad, sheep are herded with goats; cleansing judgment comes only when the earthly kingdom moves into the eternal. One is named a brother in Christ and a Catholic, as St. Ignatius of Antioch wrote centuries ago,[1] because he worships with the brothers in a Eucharist at which the Apostle-bishop preaches the Word of God and confects the Holy Sacrament. One is named a Catholic because he is a vital part of a eucharistic, priestly, worshiping assembly.

To worship, the community needs an appointed Apostle (because our worship is hierarchic); we need an offering (because our worship is priestly); we need the Word of God (because our worship is dialogue). This is basic. For our community worship act we need Word and Bread and Apostle-bishop. All of these are essentially ordered to the common worship in which we go to the Father through Christ, in whom we meet the Father in the Spirit. All are Christ's saving instruments; they exist for him, they com-

[1] *Letter to the Smyrnaeans,* VI, 8 (P.G. 5714) (New York: Fathers of the Church, Inc., 1947), p. 121.

municate his life. None of these elements is independent of him or the brothers; all interdepend, all are essentially related.[2]

Word

First in worship there is the sacred Word of God. Given high respect during the liturgical assembly in homage to the unique character of its message, the Bible brings us the living voice of God who comes to teach and inspire. In the divine Word we meet the Lord; his Spirit provokes our hearts to an ever more perfect response of commitment and faith. In Scripture we enter into a divine dialogue which creates within us a union of mind and will in preparation for a union still more profound.

Bread

Our union with Christ is established by faith in his Word; it is also made effectual by contact with his redemptive acts. And so, after the saving activity of the Word is recalled and commented on at Mass, the Eucharist takes place. It is well known that the Catholic accepts the Eucharist as the sacramental presence of the real and total Christ; he looks upon the sacred Bread as the mystery which renders present the supreme act of Sacrifice so that we, the lately come members of his Body, might identify ourselves with that saving act and participate in it as the unifying, sacramental food of our souls. To deny the Eucharist as Sacrament and Sacrifice for the Catholic is to destroy its reality and chief purpose; the Eucharist for him is the Sacrament of Christ's Sacrifice. Our Lord left his saving actions to us in the forms of fundamental human actions. These had a solidity of form that enabled them to bear the weight of greater supernatural realities that he would put into them. Thus he made the common act of cleansing into the Sacrament of Baptism. And in the Eucharist he chose Bread and Wine or the Meal as the basic sign which was to support the supernatural realities. The Eucharist renews the Last Supper; it is undoubtedly a meal. The early Church celebrated the Eucharist as a sacred Meal. Today, allowing for embellishments, the observant

---

[2] This concept is well developed by Robert W. Hovda in his chapter "What is the Church?" *Sunday Morning Crisis* (Baltimore: Helicon Press, Inc., 1963).

eye can see that the basic structure of the Mass is still that of a meal.

The Eucharistic Meal connotes feeding, and it does nourish our souls. But there is more. For Catholics it is a family meal, expressing and strengthening their family life within Christ. The Israelites looked upon the sacred meal as a sign of union with God and with each other, an enjoyment of divine favors, and a pledge of future glory and Messianic fulfillment. As a continuation of meal rites inherited from the Old Testament, the new Christian meal becomes the symbol of the family blessings of salvation, but much more. The Christian considers his Meal the fulfillment of these figure meals; a perfection and enrichment almost beyond belief.

Christ gave us the Eucharist during the week of the Pasch; in fact, he gave it to us as our Christian Pasch. And this was at the Last Supper, the most important meal in the New Testament. Like all major religious meals, there were two important actions that took place during the supper. At the start of the meal the head of the family took, blessed, and broke bread which he shared with all at table; in this way everyone present was drawn into active celebration of the feast. At the end of the meal the head of the table gave the principal festal blessing. This blessing was a thanksgiving, a eucharist, which recalled the mighty deeds which God had done for his people. On the solemn occasion of the Pasch the meal would be accompanied with a cup of blessing; after a prayer, the celebrant passed the cup to all present in order that they could echo their thanks to God for his blessings. We believe that Christ in this context of family thanksgiving, in a spirit of obedience and adoration, at the breaking of the bread told the Apostles that it was his Body and at the blessing of the cup told them that the wine was his Blood sealing the new covenant. And he invited them to share in it—a participation not only in the religious event of God-with-us, but a participation in the life of the God-Man himself; a symbol of oneness—but more, a cause of oneness with Christ.

And yet there is more. The Lord's Supper celebrated the death of Christ. His approaching death overshadowed the occasion. The Bread became his Body as *offered;* the Wine, his Blood as *shed.* In giving the Apostles his Body and Blood as food and drink Christ gave them himself also as a redeeming victim. He expressed his offering of Sacrifice in a symbolic way. He thus made his meaningful Meal more significant still; he made it the Meal of his Sacrifice. The Eucharist, the liturgy of the Body and the Blood, the Catholic believes, is the sacred Meal which makes present sacramentally the Sacrifice of Christ and feeds us on the unitive, grace-filled life of the victim of that Sacrifice. And if we ask why Christ gave us his Sacrifice in meal form, we would understand that it is because he wants us to join ourselves to it and make it our Sacrifice, our worship as well. The Sacrifice which is peculiarly his worship to the Father he has given to his worshiping Church. And in the Mass it is as head of the Mystical Body that Christ continues his priestly liturgy. The sacrificial meal from that moment until the end of time is the offering of the whole Christ, head and members —in essence we believe a perfect liturgy.

Apostle-Bishop

Our community is priestly; our worship goes to the Father through Christ, the perfect priest. Fulfilling all the prophetic figures of sacrifice, Christ accomplished his redemptive mission by the priestly offering of himself on the cross. Now as head of the Mystical Body, he lives in the Church. It is his prolongation, extension in time, his priestly body, his sacerdotal community. But in Christ's present worship of the Father, our bishop-priest or his delegate stands in a unique relation to Christ as offerer. If we are a priestly people, we might wonder why we single out one person to be our representative at worship. Christ's priestly life flows through the souls of all members of his Body, but the priesthood is not shared in the same way by all Christians. This is because the Church is hierarchical (Paul tells us that not all are Apostles, not all inspired spokesmen and teachers: I Cor 12:12ff). There are two ways in which the priesthood of Christ can be shared: by Baptism and by Holy Orders. If we distinguish two aspects of the Church, the twofold sharing of the priesthood will be easier to understand. First, the Church has official representatives of Christ. This is the hierarchy, Christ's ministerial members who are empowered and commissioned by him to make available the visible means of grace, either by the authoritative preaching of God's

Word or by the administration of his Sacraments; in short, this hierarchic priesthood visibly and authoritatively represents the invisible Christ until his Second Coming. Second, there is communion with Christ. This is the Church which lives within the priestly Christ. It is the worshiping community that he builds by grace, whose objective is to live with Christ in a union of love and prayer. The first aspect is the ministerial, hierarchical priesthood given by Holy Orders. The second aspect is the universal priesthood which makes us able to unite ourselves with Christ's Sacrifice and receive the many graces that flow from it: it is bestowed at Baptism. Nor is the latter priesthood a mere passive receptivity; it means that we actively and willingly enter into the mystery of Christ and make it our own.

Thus the Mass manifests the Church as a priestly fellowship united in Christ, praising the Father in the oneness of the Spirit and in this worship act we partake of the unifying and sanctifying life of Christ himself. In the Eucharist and the Word we have the nourishment of brotherhood, the common Meal and the common Word, ancient signs of brotherly communication and community, now made supernatural by Christ to convey his supernatural life to us. In the Apostle-bishop we have the hierarchical minister and preacher who speaks Christ's saving words and confers his sacramental mysteries.

The Church in its life, unity, and worship proclaims to the world that Christ is making good his promise to make men one as he and the Father are one. And the world at long last is slowly moving toward an analogous unity. It is beginning to sense the folly of political, social, and economic *apartheid*. Men fight for brotherhood; they rebel against imperialism and class division; they demand civil rights for all men—it would seem to give expression to an inner conviction they feel that men were not meant to be antagonists but to act in unity under God. These latter-day struggles seem the product of a subtle influence emanating from this community formed in oneness by Christ.

The Church in its unity inspires the world toward oneness and the world in turn looks to the Church to present to man a unity yet stronger, yet more vital. The Church would direct the world in its striving toward the Word, the Bread, and the Apostle-bishop.

The Catholic Church believes that Christianity must have these for fullness, for oneness—her liturgy and unity without them would be gestures only and without substance. All are related to one another and were created to capacitate the priestly community to give full worship and praise to God. With these instruments, especially in the worship act of Christians, Jesus unites and renews his community, his people, his holy Church, and brings them to God.

Chapter Two

Catholic Liturgy in History

The liturgy of the Mass is the ritual act in which the worshiping Christian assembly encounters God in Christ through Word and Sacrament. The present chapter will be a short review of the historical development of this rite. In our review we will ask ourselves some realistic questions about the Mass. In its evolution did it develop into an expressive liturgical prayer? Did the rite bring home to Christians the fact that they were in truth Christ's Mystical Body? Did the rite provide for the community a reverent, comprehensible hymn of praise to the Father? As we will see the rite in history did prove itself evocative of all these realities. In time, however, elements were introduced and undue emphases developed which tended to compromise the corporateness of the Mass. The rite, which in its early stages showed itself a hierarchic, corporate action involving everyone in the community, in time became lopsided in favor of the clerical members of the assembly. The people (in the middle ages especially) lost a sense of being a vital part of the assembly action; it so happened that events caused them to take on a detached, spectator's view. As such, the rite came in for needed reforms, and great reforms have been undertaken in our time. But first let us review these historical developments.

Two Rites

Most scholars believe that originally the Mass was two separate liturgies: one that centered around the sacred readings of the Old and New Testaments (Protestants are familiar with this liturgy also; it is their Office of the Word); the other was the rite of the Eucharist or the Lord's Supper. The former—a reading, commentary, and prayer rite—had been taken over from the religious synagogue meeting of the Jews. The Church quite probably held its synaxis liturgy on the morning of the Sabbath, giving the rite a new Christian emphasis. It began with a greeting to the assembly by the president or bishop. Lessons or readings from the Old and New Testament were read and a homily or sermon of commentary was given by the bishop. Prayers for the faithful were recited and the assembly was formally dismissed. As the Old Testament readings had been arranged to narrate the historical acts by which God had shown himself saving Lord of his people, so the New Testament selections were ordered in series to complement the already existing arrangement of readings, illustrating the life and teaching of Christ as the fulfillment of Moses and the prophets. The synaxis rite of prayer, reading, and instruction was, for early Christians, a unitive liturgy; the congregation, fed on the food of Christian truth, became more consciously one in its faith.

The liturgy of the Sacrament was of course the *re-presentation* of the Lord's Supper, the eucharistic rite left us by our Lord himself. The Eucharist was celebrated at first in conjunction with a sacred fellowship meal, or *agape,* which usually took place on Sunday evening. The local bishop, presiding in a large room or hall around an altar-table, effected the Eucharistic Mystery, using

Christ's scriptural words of institution with a few additional supplications as the consecrating, thanksgiving prayer. This Consecration and the subsequent Communion made up the substance of the Sacramental rite. In time an Offertory, a bringing of the gifts, prefaced this part of the liturgy. The Offertory was seen as a symbolic joining of ourselves to the great gift of Christ. St. Justin describes for us this early form of the eucharistic liturgy:

> Bread and chalice with wine and water are taken by the president of the brethren; he takes them, gives praise and glory to the Father in the name of the Son and of the Holy Ghost, and gives thanks at length for all the gifts we have received from Him. When he has finished the prayers and thanksgiving, the whole assembly standing by cries out in agreement: "Amen!" . . . After the president has given thanks and the people have joined in, the deacons distribute to all present the bread and the wine-and-water mixed, over which the prayer of thanksgiving has been offered.[1]

And St. John Damascene reminds us that the eucharistic liturgy, like the synaxis, is also extremely unitive in its effects.

> It is called Communion and truly is so, for by it we are made fellows of Christ, and receive of His flesh and divinity; indeed, by it we are also united and made one with each other. For since we partake of the one bread, we are all made the one body and one blood of Christ; and inasmuch as we belong to the one body of Christ, we are also members of one another.[2]

As the Church grew, separate liturgies became impractical. Also the Eucharist in its primitive association with the *agape* meal was easily abused. Paul tells the Corinthians:

> When you meet together it is no longer possible to eat the Lord's Supper . . . at the meal [*agape*] each one takes first his own supper, and one is hungry, and another drinks too much . . . my brethren, when you come together to eat, wait for one another. If anyone is hungry, let him eat at home, lest you come together unto judgment (1 Cor. 11:20-34).

---

[1] *First Apology,* c. 65, P.G., vi, 428.
[2] *The Orthodox Faith,* lib. IV, c. 13, P.G., xciv, 1153.

It would seem that Paul set in motion the steps that led to the eventual separation of the Eucharist from the abused *agape*.

Two Rites Become One

By the beginning of the second century we see that the services of Word and Sacrament were celebrated at the same time, usually on Sunday morning. The whole community joined together for this rite; it was their Mass assembly. The service was led by the bishop and his priests and deacons.[3] As president, the bishop started with a pastoral prayer for his flock. Then the priests and deacons read from the Scriptures, which the bishop subsequently explained in a homily or sermon. Responses were made by the people; prayers of intercession were said in their behalf. The rite next entered into its Sacramental phase. The Eucharist centered around an altar-table, easily visible to all. It began with a Presentation of the Gifts (later called the Offertory), then proceeded to the Thanksgiving Prayer (today called the Consecration or Canon) and concluded with the Communion and the dismissal. Both parts of the Mass—the Word and the Sacrament—came in for embellishments in future years, but the rite always remained substantially a Scripture reading and commentary service, followed by a service of Offertory, Consecration, and Communion with a dismissal.

This early Mass liturgy was conducted in the language of the people (Greek, Syriac, Coptic, etc.); Latin was used only when it became the common language of the people. The episcopal prayers which supported and gave direction to the rite were usually spontaneous. The wording was not yet set down in writing (just as the gospel was first orally preached before being written down). The only disciplinary provision was that the words used should express clearly that the service was a thanksgiving to God for his gifts, a sacramental renewing of his Sacrifice, and a reception of the gift of Christ. All was out loud and visible; the prayers and acts of the bishop and ministers were heard and seen by all. And the

[3] The early diocese was much like a parish today; the bishop was the pastor and the priests and deacons were his assistants.

words and actions were kept reverently in hand because the essential rite concerned itself always and mainly with the preaching of the Word and with Offertory, Consecration, and Communion.

Gradually prayer texts and rubrics were written down in books. As the Church spread and Christian communities grew in size, some regulation of the external expressions of the liturgy seemed necessary. Liturgical texts were prescribed by bishops, synods, and popes. These solidified into the early diocesan liturgies. As early Christians took part in these rites they were very much aware of their corporate unity with Christ and the brothers. Essential as the consecrating priest was, the Eucharist was seen as the Sacrifice of all the people. Everyone, whether cleric or layman, performed an integral part of the ceremony; all were intimately joined to Christ worshiping the Father in the Spirit. As long as the people responded at Mass in their own language and heard the Word of God and the homily of the bishop in the vernacular they retained a vivid sense of their membership in the praying and worshiping Body of Christ.

Gregory's Rite

These liturgies flourished from the third through the sixth centuries; they were flexible and underwent natural development and evolution. In the seventh century Pope Gregory made a collection of the liturgies in vogue in the western Church, which now spoke Latin as its vernacular, and from them he fashioned a liturgy for his own diocese of Rome. His rite was by no means letter perfect (some have judged it a little extravagant; some say the role of the choir was exaggerated, etc.). However, it pointed up very well the nature of the Mass as the worship of the total Christian assembly; the rite was very corporate in tone and proved exceedingly meaningful and moving to all participants. Since the rite is a high moment in the development of our present Roman Mass, it might be useful to summarize it and call attention to the elements of the rite which illustrate good pastoral service of the Christian mysteries.

The Office of the Word began with an entrance rite. The bishop and the ministers entered, accompanied by the chants of the people and the choir. Arrived at the altar, the celebrant gave his welcome to the people and offered a prayer to God for them (this comes down as the Introit and Collect of our modern Mass). Then the Scriptural dialogue with the Lord took place. Selections from the Bible were read by the lesser ministers, the subdeacon and deacon; these readings were interspersed with the responsorial chants of the people. After this, the celebrant gave a homily or sermon on the readings (here we have the Epistle, Gospel, Gradual, and Sermon of the modern Mass). When the Office of the Word was concluded, the Office of the Sacrament began. This part of the rite started with an Offertory procession; the people brought their gifts to the altar, chanting psalms as they approached the holy table. The celebrant, upon reception of these gifts, prayed over them, asking God to accept them as the symbolic commitment of the congregation to God (here we have our Offertory and Secret prayers). The Offertory was followed by the solemn Eucharistic prayer in which the gifts of bread and wine were changed into the gift of Christ. This part of the Mass was especially the province of the consecrating priest, but the people could easily identify with it. They participated by responding to the prayers of the priest; his consecrating prayer was spoken out loud and in a language they could understand. Finally, the community, having brought humble gifts to God and having been privileged to witness their miraculous consecration and conversion, after chanting the Lord's Prayer, made procession to the altar to receive God's response to their offering—Communion with the bread of Christ. During this procession the celebrant performed the rite of the "breaking of the Bread" in preparation for Communion. This portion completed, the celebrant recited a few thanksgiving prayers and the people were dismissed by the deacon (thus the modern Mass has the Consecration, the *Pater Noster,* Communion, Post-Communion and *Ite Missa Est*).

It is not difficult to see why Gregory's rite has been judged a milestone in the historical development of the Mass. For one thing, the rite did not allow the individual Christian to get lost in his own private world. He was caught up in the action and worshiped God as an integral member of Christ's Mystical Body. Christians felt that the rite was not just the action of the priest, but the prayer of all the community. The Mass, wholly audible and in the vernacular, was corporate, understandable, and meaningful. Everyone had a part and fulfilled it audibly through consecration, readings, hymns, prayers, responses, etc. As the rite unfolded it declared its purpose with clarity and impact.

Gregory's rite flourished with modifications for a few hundred years, but by the ninth century the rite in the West underwent changes in emphasis that compromised somewhat its expression as the liturgy of the total Christian assembly. From an apparent community, Mystical Body rite, where all conspired to worship as a family, the Mass became pretty much the work of the celebrating priest, his ministers, and the choir. As such, the people of God were reduced to silent and detached spectators. They began to lose vision of their place within the Christian mystery. The liturgical movement has militantly worked to restore active community to the rite; we are thankful that its work has born such amazing fruit in our time. But how did the people become corporately removed from the Mass? What made the rite so one-sidedly clerical?

Clericalization of the Mass

The history is somewhat complicated; the interplay of many forces brought about this unfortunate development. We indicate some of the more obvious factors that contributed to the "clericalization" of the rite. In the eighth and ninth centuries the Church experienced great missionary activity. The missionaries as they advanced into the North and East, faced with the problem of evangelizing primitive peoples, found the barbaric tongues a poor vehicle to express their Latin Mass rite (which by this time had a lengthy and rich tradition to endear it to the missionaries). Most settled for preaching and catechizing in the barbarous local vernaculars; the Mass itself was left in the familiar Latin.[4] Latin was exceedingly difficult for the local people to learn. Missionaries

[4] A notable exception to this procedure was the work of Saints Cyril and Methodius who missionized the primitive Slavic peoples. Assiduously ap-

sorted out the brighter converts and taught them the Latin responses, chants, etc. The processions during Mass were confined usually to those who mastered the Latin chants; the body of the convert congregation could only watch and listen. In time special Latin choirs developed, became quite expert in their singing, and composed ever more intricate chants. The people, who in time might have learned simple Latin chants, felt very much "out of it" when the musically involved Latin responses replaced the simple chants. As the chants became more complex, they took more time to sing. The celebrant was faced with much "waiting time"; to speed things up he went on with his part of the rite silently by himself. This was a practical development in an evolving rite, but as it turned out, it seems a bad one, for quiet, secret prayers, said apart from the community, are not good pastoring and helped to remove the people further from a feeling of being one with each other, one with their ministers and priests in the offering of the gifts and the reception of the gifts. People not only were deprived of their speaking parts; the parts of others were either unintelligible to them because said in a foreign tongue, or inaudible because recited in silence. In time the whole Canon of the Mass was said quietly by the celebrant; the view that equated silence with reverence gained the ascendancy.

From the ninth century on even the rites of normally "progressive" Rome were affected by this development. The Latin vernacular was in process of evolution into the Romance languages (Italian, French, Spanish, etc.); and still Latin was retained as the common liturgical language of all the West. Unfortunately this helped to remove the people further from participation. Their great liturgy prayer, the Mass, was now being said in a language which had ceased to be vernacular. The intelligentsia of clergy, monks, nobility, it is true, knew Latin and were at home with it, but the great percentage of common people did not understand it at all. It was easy to grow remote from a rite whose language was unintelligible, especially when there were no such things as printed prayer books or translation missals available.

---

plying the ancient principle that worship should be in the language of the people, they translated the liturgy into the Slavic tongue; hence, the Slavic liturgy which is still with us today.

Overloading

Another factor that made community prayer difficult was the overembellishment of the rite. This was even discernible in the rites immediately prior to Gregory's time as well as in his own liturgy. Men seem unable to leave well enough alone. They want to add to what tradition has given them; thus they make their rites sometimes more elaborate and complicated than is good for community understanding and comprehension. Embellishments are not necessarily bad, for they can indicate growth in understanding. To keep everything as austere as the early Church had it is not necessarily the ideal. When additions are made, however, they should have pastoral value; some historical insertions, as it turned out, were less pastoral than supposed. Instead of assisting comprehension and participation, many things only added to the splendor and solemnity of the rite. And after the Peace of Milan in A.D. 313, which allowed Christianity more freedom in operation, we see bigger churches being built, whose very size made for a sense of spectacle, of being *at* something rather than being *a part of* something.

In the beginning the people responded at worship in their own simple chants; this unpretentious involvement in time gave way to more complicated liturgical music with special singers. In the liturgies where bishops and the popes were celebrants the chants became almost symphonic. This was especially true in the parts where the people used to be active: the entrance rite, the Offertory and the Communion. The people, unable to participate in the musical supports to these rites, surrendered their role to the choir.

Fore Mass

The Fore Mass had as its rallying point the reading of the Word followed by a sermon or homily commentary; the people responded by attentive listening which gave rise to prayers and hymns of praise, thanksgiving, and petition. In time this rite inflated to the point where the Word of God was only one of a number of things done in the Fore Mass; this put the central importance of the office of readings out of focus. The Introit, Kyrie, Gloria, Creed (sung with intricate solemnity) took on great importance and became almost as sacred as the Word. The hymns and chants were intended to rally within the people a responsive spirit; but the result in time was that the proclamation of the Word became lost in a profusion of chants and prayers added to an originally simple outline. Doubtless larger congregations needed more prayer responses to feel vitally involved in the Mass. The idea of participation is good, but when it became obvious that the Word was being submerged, the rite should have been disciplined to put the emphasis where it was due: on the proclamation of the Word.

Perhaps the most regrettable example of inflation (here and in the remaining parts of the liturgy) was the role of the celebrant. In the beginning the priest as representative of Christ was the catalyst uniting all in corporate worship before the Father. Everyone contributed an integral part of the worship prayer: the celebrant spoke in the people's name, preached and consecrated; the lectors read the lessons of the Old Testament and the letters of the Apostles; the deacons proclaimed the Gospel, and the singers and the faithful chanted in response. Each segment of the assembly had its distinct ritual book to indicate its part in the community worship action. But as the rite evolved the functions of various members of the community were said and done also by the priest; in time these community roles were given over almost wholly to the celebrant. The hierarchic structure of the Fore Mass was thus compromised; everything was done by the president, all roles were his. It seemed bad pastoral practice to destroy the tangible sign of the assembly structure of the Church by letting the celebrant usurp the roles of others.

And, like the Fore Mass, the Eucharistic part of the liturgy (Offertory, Consecration and Communion) also experienced its share of embellishments.

Offertory

It is true that everything (every symbolic action and spoken word of the Mass) can be sanctified and sanctifying. There is nothing that God cannot use for his purposes, but there are different levels of importance; God himself has put a hierarchy of values in creation and man should respect it. Sometimes, however, man forgets this hierarchy. For example, he unwittingly put many actions in the Mass on the same plain. Placing wine into the chalice cup, purifying one's hands, kissing the altar: these certainly do not have the importance of the key ritual actions of the Consecration and Communion. But as the Mass evolved a solemn reverence surrounded these lesser Offertory actions; so much so that in time the climactic moments of the liturgy of the Eucharist did not stand out. The Offertory had a simple purpose: to place the bread and the wine on the altar in preparation for the Eucharistic Consecration and Communion. But the Church sought to use the action as a means of personal identification with Christ's coming Offering. In the fifth century she introduced the Offertory procession in which the faithful brought gifts to the altar. The pastoral significance of this procession was real. The believer is an offerer; he has a duty to offer himself to the Father in union with Christ. In the procession the Christian could show the real connection between himself and Christ and his coming Offering. This procession of the people toward the altar was accompanied by meaningful chants. The priest received the gifts of the people in silence; at the conclusion of the procession, the celebrant blessed the people's offering with a prayer. Up to this point the rite had great pastoral value. The bringing of the gifts was not considered a ritual offering; the Consecration made clear that only Christ is our ritual Offering. As time went by, however, many prayers were recited in connection with every Offertory action and unfortunately most were said quietly by the priest; again it seemed the celebrant was off by himself performing rites the community was not to intrude on. There were special prayers for the oblation of the bread, the consecration of the water, the oblation of the wine, the incensing of the altar, the lavabo, etc. All of these additional prayers became sacrosanct and were fixed as part of the western rite in the sixteenth century. Expansion of this rite thus became overly elaborate and pastorally confusing. In time some people thought the Eucharist had two major parts: the offering of the laity, and the offering of Christ—the composite of the two being the Mass. The simplicity of the primitive rite and of the one next introduced, consisting of the procession with chants and a concluding prayer, helped to bring out the meaning of the Offertory: the joining of the people to the Offering of Christ at Mass. The subsequent extravagant inflation of the rite was confusing. In the Mass there is one single offering, Christ's; our action is only valid because it moves toward his oblation.

Consecration

The Consecration also suffered an inflated expansion. The rite derives from the Jewish benediction service which was made up of sacred greetings and an exclamatory prayer to God, an *anamnesis* (re-presentation) of God's great deeds for his people and a summary hymn of praise for his mighty acts on their behalf. This rite issued in a prayer of thanksgiving and supplication, for what God has done inspires our hope that he will do still greater things for us. The early rites of the Christian Canon show this order. Note the words of the *Apostolic Tradition of St. Hippolytus*:

> 4. We render thanks unto thee, O God, through Thy Beloved Child Jesus Christ, Whom in the last times Thou didst send to us [to be] a Savior and Redeemer and the Messenger of Thy counsel; 5. Who is Thy Word inseparable, through Whom Thou madest all things and in Whom Thou wast well pleased; 6. Whom Thou didst send from heaven into the Virgin's womb and Who conceived within her was made flesh and demonstrated to be Thy Son being born of the Holy Spirit and a Virgin; 7. Who fulfilling Thy will and preparing for Thee a holy people stretched forth His hands for suffering that He might release from suffering them who have believed in Thee; 8. Who when He was betrayed to voluntary suffering that He might abolish death and rend the bond of the devil and tread down hell and enlighten the righteous and establish the ordinance and demonstrate the resurrection: 9. Taking bread and making eucharist [i.e., giving thanks] to Thee said: Take eat: this is my Body which is broken for you. Likewise also the cup, saying: this is my Blood which is shed for you. 10. When ye do this, ye do my "anamnesis." 11. Doing therefore the "anamnesis" of His death and resurrection we offer to Thee the bread and the cup making eucharist to Thee . . . 12. And we pray Thee that . . . Thou wouldst grant to all Thy saints who partake to be united

> to Thee that they may be fulfilled with the Holy Spirit for the confirmation of their faith and in truth. . . .[5]

By the fifth century there is an inflation when mention of the names of the living (the diptychs) was inserted before the Consecration. It was fitting to mention the community and its needs in the Eucharistic part of the Mass, but it seems more logical to do this after the Consecration; then our brother Christ is sacramentally present and can more efficaciously take our needs to the Father. The supplication before seemed to interrupt the early Canon in its movement toward the prayer which rendered present our eternal Sacrifice.

By the twelfth century the elevation of the host was introduced, and sometime later the chalice. Unfortunately by this time the rite had become quite predominantly the work of the celebrating priest. The people, no longer participating vitally in the assembly prayer, at least wanted to see and adore the present Christ. The Church acquiesced to this desire; certainly the doctrine of the real presence was avowed by such an elevation. Still the gesture broke up the unity of the Canon, replacing its "offertory" character with a tone of veneration for the real presence.[6] The "adoration" elevation upset the order of the Eucharistic prayer as it moved toward the doxology, a hymn of praise during which the priest, in a gesture of offering, elevated the host and chalice together, saying:

> Through Christ all these good gifts created by you, Lord, are by you sanctified, endowed with life, blessed and bestowed upon us. Through him, and with him, and in him, may you, God the Father Almighty, in the unity of the Holy Spirit, have all honor and glory forever. (Concluding prayer of Roman Canon)

The doxology was to be the climactic and eloquent conclusion of the Canon, expressing how the redemption, sacramentalized in the signs of Bread and Wine, had re-established men in the true and full praise of God's glory. This significant prayer and elevation,

[5] Paul F. Palmer, *Sources of Christian Theology, Vol. I, Sacraments and Worship* (Westminster, Md.: The Newman Press, 1955), pp. 41-42.

[6] In simple minds the gesture often gave grounds for an imagined magical Eucharist.

however, had been somewhat eclipsed by the "adoration" elevation of the Consecration.

Communion

The Communion rite of the Eucharist also underwent some inflationary evolution. In the beginning the main business of the rite was to "break the holy bread" and for the people to come reverently to the altar to receive the supernatural gift of Christ. The Our Father was introduced quite early and was a most fitting inclusion. Other prayers were recited at the *fraction* and preparatory Communion prayers were introduced. None of these additions took away from the assembly nature of the rite as such. But as time went on the priest said all of the prayers himself and usually in a quiet voice. As the faithful did not participate, it induced in them a listening, spectator attitude. In the early Communion rites, all participated and chanted together as they approached the altar in procession. In time the procession was eliminated and the faithful, if they came to Communion at all, approached the altar silently in abstract, individualistic fashion. By the early middle ages, intinction (the sacred host dipped in the sacred wine) had become the mode of reception; this was adopted out of a motive of cleanliness. As the bread began to crumble, intinction became undesirable and Communion under the sign of bread only became the custom. And because the faithful received Communion so rarely (they viewed the Sacrament more as Christ's presence to be honored than as a re-presentation of his Sacrifice to which they must actively adhere), the Lateran Council in the thirteenth century made yearly Communion obligatory.

Such a state of affairs would not have developed if the Church had preached more earnestly and lived more openly the doctrine of the Mystical Body. As we have seen, in the early forms of the Mass, the people were integrally involved in every phase; no prayer or reading went without its response from the people. The Mass was not a monologue but a community dialogue. And Communion was seen as the climax toward which the entire rite moved. But by the late middle ages the contrast could not be more regrettable. The Mass was almost completely a clerical prayer. At the Canon especially, the celebrant stood in solemn isolation before God; the people could only busy themselves with their own private prayers and devotions (and these became quite individualistic). The inner meaning of the Mass as a corporate prayer was difficult to discern; the language barrier and the increased use of silent prayer had rendered its meaning remote. And Holy Communion was seen as a reality more to be adored than received. What brought about the eclipse of the doctrine of the mystical oneness of all of us in Christ?

Christ's Mystical Oneness with Men Understressed

Many reasons may be educed; the important one seems to be that because Christological heresies were at work in the Church, she was forced to stress above all else the divinity of Christ.[7] It is certainly true that a "super" reverence for our Lord as God resulted from the Church's efforts to counteract Arianism. This heresy, perhaps the most far reaching in the history of the Church, flatly denied Christ's divinity. Its influence on the Church lasted for centuries, so much so that the Church, at the risk of losing countless numbers of the faithful, had to set Christ's divinity before the people in unmistakable terms. This regretfully resulted in a diminution of emphasis on his humanity. When Christ is preeminently divine, the Mystical Body, our status of oneness with him, our head, our priest, our way to the Father, becomes obscured. Certainly there was no want of orthodoxy in stressing his divinity. Still the stress put the total mystery of Christ a bit out of focus. When one truth is taught almost exclusively, related truths tend to become blurred, and this was the case with Christ's humanity. The stress had its effect on the liturgy.

If we consider Christ exclusively as divine, we can easily lose sight of the fact that he did not become one of us primarily to solicit adoration. He came to capacitate a fallen race for redemption; he became our brother to lead us in forgiveness and worshipful submission back to the Father. Certainly Christ deserves

[7] Godfrey Diekmann, "Popular Participation and the History of Christian Piety," in *Come, Let Us Worship* (Baltimore: Helicon Press, Inc., 1961).

worship; but as our redeemer (and that is the office that he preeminently fulfills at Mass) he is one of us, living in us and serving us, as he told us himself: "I am here among you as your servant" (Lk 22:27). But in its efforts to crush Arian influence the Church inadvertently minimized Christ's humanity. In this connection Karl Adam has reflected:

> Christ no longer stands by man's side as the representative and advocate of mankind; and he as the man, Christ Jesus, and the First-born of his brethren, no longer offers the sacrifice of mankind to the triune God. He has, so to speak, crossed over, and is now on God's side, and himself is the awful and unapproachable God.[8]

Christ became a transcendent Lord working his redemption from afar through his priests. Through their power the divine Christ was rendered present for adoration. The whole idea of the worshiping assembly of the Lord—that through and with and in Christ all of us were being brought to the Father—this idea practically disappeared. The Canon of the Mass in time became an inner temple to which only the ordained priest was fit to enter. There were even introduced into the Mass private prayers designed solely for the priest. In the Canon, prayers of corporate offering were replaced by prayers of the celebrating priest to which the people had to identify as they could. There was no denial that the Mass was the Sacrifice of the Mystical Christ, head and members. But the fact is, the theology of the Mass as mystical assembly offering was not stressed; certainly it was not understood by most of the faithful.

And if such a disproportionate stress on Christ's divinity had not been allowed to influence the expression of the Mass, there would be no such thing as a vernacular problem, which was discussed earlier in this chapter. When Latin grew incomprehensible to the common people it should have been dropped in favor of the local vernacular. It was retained and little serious objection was raised because people were confused about their rights to understand the rite and to take part in it. A psychological wall had been

---

[8] *Christ Our Brother* (New York: Sheed & Ward, 1931), p. 49.

erected between priest and people that has only recently been removed.

Still the Eucharist, the Mass, remained central to Catholic life; it always has and always will. It is true that the rite was not overtly a very corporate action where people could sense their assembly within Christ; it was more a gathering to witness the appearance of God among his people. The history of the middle ages shows that much of the piety of the faithful focused on the vision of the host (e.g., processions, expositions of the Blessed Sacrament, etc.). These devotions were usually theologically sound; still it must be admitted that at times there was much in them that bordered on superstition.

Eucharistic piety was closely linked with our Lord's passion. This was good and praiseworthy; it was not, however, always associated with our own active and intelligent identification with the Offering of Christ, our victim priest. And, as stated earlier, when the faithful withdrew from active participation in the Mass, they received Holy Communion much more rarely. The Sacrament of intimate union with Christ and the brethren gave place to the Sacrament of God's epiphany where men came to bow in adoration, pleading mercy for their sins.

A regrettable condition, then, of pre-Reformation times was the lack of awareness on the part of many of the faithful that they were Christ's Mystical Body. The Church was looked on more as a human organization, established by Christ, given assistance and protection by him, but not unmistakably his incarnate extension in time. The Church exercised Christ's authority in order to secure moral order and virtue on earth. This authority of course was identified particularly with the clerical rulers of the Church. In fact, the living, active, worshiping Church was equated all too often with its clerical members; the laity were simply to receive, to obey, to learn. If Christians sought grace from Christ, more often than not it was a petition for his actual grace (a help to do his will); sanctifying grace (living with the life of Christ himself) was not fully understood or appreciated. Instead of considering themselves God's holy people who lived joyously within Christ in union with the brethren, the faith became a system of "do's and don'ts" done out of loyalty to Christ's moral dictates. And if Christianity is only loyalty to Christ's commandments, the faith is easily reducible to morality and the Church to a moral system. And this moralistic climate influenced the development and understanding of the Mass.

It became a work to be done out of loyalty to Christ or as a work which gained actual graces. The efficaciousness of this "work" *ex opere operato* was stressed by pre-Reformation theologians; this emphasis minimized in many minds the necessity of praying the Mass *ex opere operantis* (i.e., giving one's personal, fervent response through acts and prayers of faith, hope, love, etc.). The Mass became for many exclusively an instrument for receiving God's blessing, spiritual and temporal. Without doubt the Mass in the late middle ages had fallen on bad days.

We find, however, in the centuries immediately preceding the Protestant Reformation attempts to bring about reforms. For example, efforts were made to correct abuses and to help people understand what was taking place at Mass. A full generation before Luther there appeared a number of prayer books written for the laity; these gave translations of the Ordinary of the Mass (the parts that remain the same each day) as well as the Propers (the changeable parts) of the major feasts. These books were an effort to increase the understanding, faith, and participation of the laity. Even in the century of the Reformation a liturgical reform movement was at work, but Luther identified with it, and of course this forestalled the Church's embracing of the movement for many years. Many individual theologians and priests, even diocesan synods in several countries, inveighed against the abuses that surrounded the Mass. The fathers of Trent were no less severe in their condemnation: "Among the causes which have contributed to the general weakening of the efficacy of the Mass . . . two stand out most strongly—superstition and avarice." [9] The Council recommended the reduction of votive Masses which had been the source of superstitious abuse. Masses generally were to be confined in number; too many celebrations easily gave rise to contempt. The missal was reformed; the Offertory procession was eliminated

---

[9] *Sacrosancti et Oecumenici Concilii Trindentini* (Brioci, ex Typis Prud'-homme, 1823), pp. 207-8.

because superstitions had also been associated with it. In the chaos of the Reformation, however, Trent had to defend the doctrine of the clerical priesthood as well as the doctrine of the Mass as a Sacrifice; both of these had been denied. Since the Mass was being attacked, the Council felt constrained to stabilize the rubrics of the Mass in view of future analytic reforms. The Mass in essence was thus preserved; but the Mass as a comprehensible instrument of worship was encased in a rite badly in need of reform.

Luther claimed the papists taught that the Mass produced its effect automatically and that the personal piety and participation of those attending added little to its value. He called for the people to bring fervor and personal commitment to the Mass. Such teaching was in many ways to the point. And it is easy to see why his preaching appealed so powerfully to ordinary people, why it aroused within them a spirit of renovation and personal love for Christ. His call for personal involvement in the liturgy was a sound Catholic principle that needed preaching; that he would stress it out of all proportion and divorce it from the other valid principle of *ex opere operato* was, of course, most regrettable to Catholics.

In little more than a generation Christians became hardened in division. This was especially discernible at worship. The Mass was rejected by many as an unsuitable liturgy. To them it meant only superstition and avarice; indeed in its clericalized, Latinized form it seemed to have lost all relevancy.

If the Mass had been understood, if the faithful had been taught to see it as the Offering of the Mystical Christ in whom and with whom they lived out their lives of commitment, faith and grace, the Protestant Reformation could not have happened, at least not with such terribly divisive consequences. Indeed, the Reformation was a judgment on the pastoral mission of the Church. The people rejected only what they did not understand, what they did not feel was truly theirs. But with judgment came grace to reform and we have seen this grace produce marvelous renewal in the worship life of the Church. And it is remarkable that a Lutheran theologian of our day, Hans Asmussen, in the context of the papal encyclical, *Mediator Dei,* would state that none of the traditional arguments of Protestants against the Mass is still valid.

We can learn a powerful lesson from the historical evolution of the Mass. We believed in Christ; we obscured our vision of him as Lord, as Head, as Priest in worship, but we have been restored to a fuller and clearer vision of who he is and who we are within him. In this century especially, all the popes and the Second Vatican Council have proclaimed clearly the identity of Christ with his people and in a manner and with an emphasis that has reached the consciousness of great masses of the faithful. We rejoice that in our day we are witnessing a great renewal in the liturgical life of the Church; it is bringing home to us the truth that we are a community within Christ and are especially united with him and with each other when we join him in the mystical Offering of the Mass.

Chapter Three

Catholic Liturgy in Renewal

Salvation History has shown us the great acts by which God has redeemed us. History is rich in narrative to tell us what our saving God has done for his people and promises yet to do for us. This history also reveals the response of men to God's saving deeds. Sometimes that history is written large and generous; at other times man's response has been hesitating, selfish, or indifferent. The history of the liturgy of the Mass, the Catholic's worship response to God, is no exception. Men have used the rite in praise of God as their most sacred, corporate prayer; they have also allowed the rite to become remote and incomprehensible to the people, a prayer that at times made corporate worship very difficult. This is the more alarming when we realize that Catholics should believe that the substantive portion of their liturgy is the actual prayer of Christ-with-and-in-us and is the main source of extending the fruits of his redemptive deeds in time. This rite is not only the great worshiping prayer of Catholics; it is their grace-filled encounter with God in Christ. They should make it a conscious community gathering in the Lord; they should preserve and develop it as their most meaningful and attractive source of grace.

We have seen the historical evolution of the Mass rite. There was much in its development that was good and pastoral. There was much also that was not so pastoral. The evolution of the Mass saw the rite add and absorb elements which as time advanced called for change and purgation, and we are witnessing in our day the fruitful results of a movement that has worked hard and successfully to bring about needed reforms in the Mass. The sum of the forces which have brought this about is called the liturgical movement.

Until recently many looked upon liturgists as theological liberals who wanted to carry the Church down an uncertain, untried path; others dismissed them as esoteric hobbyists who had fallen in love with ancient ceremonies, rubrics, and chants and who wanted to wish on the Church more esthetic rites from the "romantic" past. Nothing could be further from the truth. The liturgical movement is not nostalgia or romantic estheticism; it is not a strange new approach to the faith. It concerns itself with the basic, ordinary life of the Church. Essentially it proclaims that Christians join in supernatural community to perform, each according to his station within Christ, the ordinary and essential actions that pertain to them as Christians. Liturgy, this movement believes, is not something one can take or leave—it is of the essence of Christian life; without it there would be no full Christian life. The movement does not deny the mystery and sacredness of the Mass, but it does want to bring home to Christians that the rite is their distinctive Christian act, their most necessary and corporate act, the root response that they as the divinely formed assembly of God give to his redemption.

Liturgy, as J. A. Jungmann points out,[1] is not an arbitrary part

[1] *Pastoral Liturgy* (New York: Herder & Herder, Inc., 1962), pp. 89-101, 368-87.

of Christian life; it is essential and as such must be our most pastoral concern. And if the liturgy is to be reformed, it will be in the light of pastoral significance. As we have seen, a long and involved history has gone into the formation of our present liturgy. But what distinguished and directed this development? What was the key factor that explained the creation of new liturgical forms and the many changes in liturgical rites? The force that motivated all these changes—even though our hindsight shows us that blunders were made along the way—was the Church's effort to fulfill her pastoral worshiping mission. And pastoral concern is the motivating force that inspires the modern liturgical movement. The movement, therefore, is not a giving in to nostalgia but a practical effort which is working to renew the lives of all the faithful here and now through a revived liturgy. But we must confess that before the movement became universally pastoral in its apostolate, there were some inauspicious beginnings that compromised somewhat its reforming purpose and which in their esoteric and antiquarian turns have given the movement an exclusivist reputation against which liturgists still have to defend themselves.

The movement, now thoroughly pastoral, has undergone roughly three stages, dating from the middle of the nineteenth century. One can of course say that there were reform efforts under way long before this, but all of these proved short-lived. It is sufficient to note that the eighteenth and nineteenth centuries saw the beginning of studies which when brought to a more fruitful development in our time were to provide a scholarly and traditional base for the present liturgical movement; the reference here of course is to the renewal of historical inquiries, patristic and liturgical studies, which were to reveal the permanent factors that underlie the liturgy, allowing us to discern the passing pastoral from the permanently pastoral. In these studies the Church came to see that the substantive elements of the Mass were always retained, but in their retention were adapted to the mentality and culture of the time; a static permanency of expression was not a virtue at all but a frustration really of the living and growing nature of the Church and its worship.

Dom Guéranger

But the movement in its present form dates by way of preface to the work inaugurated by Dom Guéranger, abbot of the monastery of Solesmes. Many liturgical scholars have seen his work more a hindrance to renewal than a help. Though much of the criticism is deserved, it seems a little excessive. Admitting that his ideas were not universally appropriate, it seems unfair to dismiss his movement as solely antiquarian and esthetical as many have done. More accurately, it was a little above the common life of the Church; in its monastic setting it never reached the workaday Christian. Dom Guéranger tried to awaken his monks to the doctrinal and devotional riches of the liturgy; he wanted to make the Mass a meaningful, living prayer, the root source of Christian grace. To do this he thought it necessary to go back to the past, to what he considered to be a more living and ideal tradition. The main difficulty was that he lacked the historical documents that would have enabled him to discern what was "essential" in the past rites of history and what was only "temporary and peripheral." His renewal went back to a time when the Roman liturgy was not at its best (here again we judge him by hindsight); in fact, it settled on the Gothic period when the liturgy, though beautiful to see and hear, was not fully corporate in expression. His return to the past was thus more of a cultural restoration than an authentic pastoral renewal addressed to God's universal flock in their present condition. Because of this, its reforms reached groups of the *initiated* rather than ordinary Christians. The splendor of his restored liturgy with its revival of purified Gregorian chant inspired estheticians, the learned, spiritual people who wished for a less emotional piety, but the average Catholic was not much affected by it.

Pius X and Dom Lambert Beauduin

Dom Guéranger's work was followed by a second, more practical stage. The remarkable Dom Lambert Beauduin of Belgium sponsored a truly pastoral liturgical movement that was to have wide influence on the Church. But before Dom Lambert inaugurated his liturgical apostolate, the reforms of Pius X at the beginning of this century paved a way toward renewal by revitalizing certain aspects of the Church's worship and sacramental life. Many in fact would date the "official" beginning of the present liturgical movement from the pontificate of Pius X. Moved by a keen pastoral sense, he wanted Christians to look on themselves as a community within Christ and to see the liturgy as the most sacred and distinctive prayer of that community. He enunciated the principle that has been repeatedly quoted as the basis for sound liturgical reform: ". . . the first and necessary font of a truly Christian spirit for the faithful is their active participation in the most holy and sacred mysteries and in the solemn and common prayer of the Church." The liturgy, he said, is not only to be seen and heard, but to be participated in, bringing "before God the whole individual man in the whole Christian community." In this connection he urged that the people's responsive parts at high Mass be given back to them. He also undertook the correction and development of the texts and rites of worship and the reform of church music. He changed the established custom that delayed first Communion until adolescence, insisting on early and frequent reception of the Sacrament. He began efforts to bring balance to the Church's calendar; in the future, Sundays, the Lenten season, the feasts of Christ were to take precedence over the feasts of the saints in the liturgical year. He began the purification and simplification of the rites of the Mass and the Sacraments.[2]

Renewal, however, is not automatically effected by papal decrees, and for the flowering of the movement as a pastoral phenomenon, we must refer to the work of the Belgian monk, Dom Lambert Beauduin. Dom Lambert viewed the Church as a living mystery, a divinely formed worshiping community, the true Body of the Mystical Christ. To him liturgical life, worship life, was the vital center of Christian life itself. As priest, monk, and theologian he was convinced that the solid base of the Church's spirit-

---

[2] Much of this work was temporarily tabled after Pius' death. The reform was continued actively again by Pius XII. And in the meantime the liturgical movement through study, instruction, and active participation was growing steadily toward maturity.

ual life and the fundamental catechesis of the Christian faith are to be found in the liturgy. And this is true for all Christians, not just the chosen (monastic) few. He wanted Catholics to find in their parish church and its liturgical life the epicenter of the Christian life itself. Their parish priest was not to be seen as a local Church governor, but as the man who leads, teaches, blesses, and sanctifies them in Christ's name. The parish Mass was to be reverenced as the great assembly meeting of God's people where, through the action of the visible priesthood, men, already joined in ties of fraternity were steadily converted into a fuller sharing of Christ and a deeper fraternity with each other. Dom Lambert referred frequently to the words of Pius X, that the spirit of Christianity is to be enkindled within the souls of men. Liturgy is to evoke and foster this spirit; to this end all the faithful must be allowed ". . . active participation in the most holy and sacred mysteries and in the solemn and common prayer of the Church." In active liturgical participation Catholics will discover the Christian life; here they will be graced to carry out the Christian mission.

Dom Lambert put forward his program of liturgical renewal at the Catholic Congress of Malines in 1909. From then until his death in 1960 through his writing, teaching, pastoral institutes, and retreats, he worked for ever more widespread reform on the pastoral level. His disciples grew steadily in number and the apostolate took root in most countries of the world.

In his efforts to reform liturgical practice, Dom Lambert was no radical. He was well aware that the present Roman rite needed reform, but he refused to return to unfamiliar rites or to introduce doubtfully valid experiments. He kept the rite as it was and sought to reform it. The liturgy, after all, is the property of the Church; it is a "given factor" as A. Nocent reminds us.[3] We should accept it as a treasure from the Church and aim our efforts at knowing and understanding it, of performing it as intelligently as we can. When we perfect what we have, then we can entertain suitable changes. The liturgical movement of Dom Lambert thus

---

[3] *The Future of the Liturgy* (New York: Herder & Herder, Inc., 1963), pp. 32-45, 102-11.

never gave into romantic antiquarianism or wild innovationism. The movement sought rather to rediscover the living spirit of the past and to make it a conscious actuality in the Church of today. The liturgical life of the Church abounds with riches as yet not fully realized; it is wiser not to add to or subtract from the liturgy until we have fully explored and put to use its present fruits.

Two means used by Dom Lambert to restore understanding, participation, and community to the liturgy proved quite successful. They were the introduction of good vernacular missals with commentaries and the use of the dialogue community Mass. By these instruments he managed to restore a degree of corporateness to the liturgy and made the "we" of the Mass meaningful again to the faithful. Priest and congregation were brought closer together; the people no longer felt passively removed from the actions and prayers which took place at the altar. The doctrine of the lay priesthood became an active belief in the Church again.

Maria Laach

The liturgical movement also owes much of its success to work which went on in Germany about this same time. There we discover another liturgical reformer in the person of Dom Ildefons Herwegen, abbot of Maria Laach. His concern at first was not with a universal pastoral apostolate like Dom Lambert; he wanted primarily to intensify the spiritual and community life of his own monastery. In this effort he centered the intellectual and spiritual life of the abbey around the liturgy, for it was conceived as the most powerful instrument for effecting spiritual and corporate unity. Maria Laach did achieve a remarkable community of the spirit and the abbey exercised a wide influence on the Church throughout Germany. The monastery made an immeasurable contribution to the liturgical movement in its scholarly liturgical studies; these produced a wealth of material from which liturgists found ample historical justification for their pleas for reform. In this connection, we note the provocative works of Dom Odo Casel. We may have some reservations about accepting his "theology of mysteries,"[4] at least in the form he expressed it, but no one can say that his thoughts on the liturgy did not bring to the surface profound insights which have brought new life to the theology of the Sacraments, the Eucharist especially.

Biblical Renewal

Nor can we overlook the scriptural and patristic scholarship that assisted the movement in this and other centers in Germany and Austria and later in France. Pius Parsch sponsored a successful liturgical renewal in Austria that restored to the liturgy a strong reverence for the Bible. He saw the ongoing biblical renewal as a strong ally to liturgical renewal, for both established clearly the nature of the Church as a worshiping assembly. The biblical revival, of course, reached ever greater proportions, and it was extremely appropriate that liturgical celebrations under Parsch's direction gave Scripture a prominence that helped the faithful to focus their attention on its fuller and deeper meaning. And so the apostolates of Maria Laach and those of Parsch and others developed side by side it seemed providentially, for it is only in and through each other—a new understanding of the Word and a deeper realization of the Eucharistic Mystery—that Christian worship can rightly be understood as the distinctive act of the living Church. And we are presently rejoicing in the fact that the liturgical and biblical renewals have given rise to a whole new doctrinal renewal in the Church. Our theology is taking on a biblical and liturgical emphasis and expression; it is becoming more positive in tone, less defensive and polemical in formulation. And this doctrinal renewal has in its turn heightened the move toward liturgical reform.

De Facto Liturgical Reform

And now in the context of pastoral renewal we come to the third phase of the liturgical movement, the stage of liturgical re-

[4] *The Mystery of Christian Worship* (Westminster, Md.: The Newman Press, 1962).

form itself. Historical studies (doctrinal, liturgical, and pastoral) made it quite clear that our present liturgy was not in the best of health. These studies gave the full historical picture of the development of the liturgy and scholars were able to determine the factors that contributed to the decline of the liturgy as an active influence on Christian life. It became clear that if the liturgy was to return to its rightful place in the life of the Church, reforms had to be effected. Historical scholarship made it easier to see which reforms would be in keeping with the purpose of liturgy, which changes would be more truly pastoral in the light of the past traditions of the Church, and which might be prompted by some modern urge for novelty. Certainly there was no desire to restore ancient liturgical practice as such. The reformers sought to discover the living quality in past liturgical traditions and to restore that quality to our modern liturgy in such a way that it would be vital and meaningful for the members of the Church today. Charles Davis shows that the Church in her effort to renew doctrine has often, in the context of the contemporary needs of the Church, returned to the living past in this way.

> A doctrine is renewed by reflection on the past tradition of the Church and by reaching beyond more recent formulations. A striking example of this is the modern renewal in our understanding of the Church. Owing to the need to combat various errors, attention was concentrated for centuries on the Church as a visible and hierarchical society. This one-sidedness has been overcome by going back to the earlier tradition and digging out the rich data found there on the other aspects of the Church [e.g., its Mystical Body, worshiping assembly aspects, etc.]. It is the same with liturgical renewal: a return to tradition to overcome defects of the present. Pastoral necessity shows the need for reform. Historical study, doctrinal reflection, and pastoral experience, all help to determine its direction. It was in that way that the new order of Holy Week was achieved—an order which is both ancient and new, a restoration, yet one adapted to present pastoral needs.[5]

The liturgical movement had created a new love for the Mass and had provided the necessary insights to fire the desire for its

[5] *Liturgy and Doctrine* (New York: Sheed & Ward, 1960), p. 19.

reform. And recent popes and the Second Vatican Council have decreed reforms and set in motion the steps that will effect other desirable changes in the liturgy itself. Pius XII certainly will be remembered as a liturgical reformer. His encyclical, *Mystical Body* (*Mystici Corporis*), was a classical restatement of an ancient truth which must stand at the base of any successful liturgical reform. And he gave official approval to the theory of a renewed worship in his great encyclical letter, *On the Liturgy* (*Mediator Dei*). The latter document clearly proclaimed Christ as our priestly mediator between God and man. And Christian worship, performed representatively by the priests and people of the Church, was declared to be the essential instrument that perpetuates Christ's redemptive work of mediation in time.

The liturgy had remained almost static for four hundred years. Pius X called for renewal. Pius XII answered the pleas of bishops, pastors, and scholars in a practical way. Relaxing the discipline that governed reception of Holy Communion, he made the Sacrament easier to approach. He again allowed the celebration of evening Mass. Modern languages in the Mass and the Sacraments were permitted. He established a commission to reform service books (missals, breviary, ritual, etc.). He instituted simpler, clearer forms of the main feasts of the Christian year: the Easter celebration (1951) and Holy Week (1956); through these reformed rites the people were again officially involved in the liturgy through communal prayers and hymns. And of course, more, much more was in store. John XXIII called his Council. Its purpose was to renew the Church, to bring the Church up to date, to attend to the pastoral needs of the faithful in this age, and this certainly implied the pastoral reform of the liturgy.

The Council indeed was John's idea, but the Spirit that prompted him to call it was the same Spirit that had sowed the seeds for its pastoral *aggiornamento* many years before in the liturgical, biblical, and doctrinal studies and renewals of the men mentioned above. This is more than obvious as the Council has officially adopted the apostolate of the liturgical reform and has decreed renewal in light of the scholarly and pastoral works of these men. In *The Constitution on the Sacred Liturgy* of the Second Vatican Council one can certainly hear echoes of Beauduin,

Herwegen, Casel, Parsch, Jungmann, and many other of the great liturgical reformers. As someone has said: the document not only sounds like a liturgist's plea; it looks very much like his homework. This document contains so much of what the reformers were working for and includes so many of their insights and suggested reforms that it might be well to cite the more important parts of it as a summary of the principles and applications of liturgical renewal in our time.

Introduction: This sacred Council has several aims in view: it desires to impart an ever increasing vigor to the Christian life of the faithful; to adapt more suitably to the needs of our own times those institutions which are subject to change; to foster whatever can help to call the whole of mankind into the household of the Church. The Council therefore sees particularly cogent reasons for undertaking the reform and promotion of the liturgy. 2. For the liturgy . . . most of all . . . the divine sacrifice of the eucharist, is the outstanding means whereby the faithful may express in their lives, and manifest to others, the mystery of Christ and the real nature of the true Church . . . the liturgy daily builds up those who are within [the Church] into a holy temple of the Lord, into a dwelling place for God in the Spirit (Eph 2:21-22), to the mature measure of the fullness of Christ (Eph 4:13) [and] at the same time . . . marvelously strengthens their power to preach Christ, and thus shows forth the Church to those who are outside as a sign lifted up among the nations (Isa 11:12) under which the scattered children of God may be gathered together until there is one sheepfold and one shepherd (John 10:16).

Chapter I: General Principles for the Renewal and Promotion of the Sacred Liturgy:

A. The Nature of the Sacred Liturgy and its Importance in the Church's Life:

7. . . . the liturgy is considered as an exercise of the priestly office of Jesus Christ . . . in the liturgy the whole public worship is performed by the Mystical Body of Christ, that is, by the head and his members.

From this it follows that every liturgical celebration, because it is an action of Christ the priest and of his Body which is the Church, is a sacred action surpassing all others . . .

10. . . . the liturgy is the summit toward which the activity of the Church is directed; at the same time it is the font from which all her power flows. For the aim and object of apostolic works is that all who are made sons of God by faith and baptism should come together to praise God in the midst of his Church, to take part in the sacrifice, and to eat the Lord's Supper.

The liturgy in its turn moves the faithful, filled with the "paschal sacraments," to be "one in holiness"; it prays that "they may hold fast in their lives to what they have grasped by their faith"; the renewal in the eucharist of the covenant between the Lord and man draws the faithful into the compelling love of Christ and sets them on fire. From the liturgy, therefore, and especially from the eucharist, as from a font, grace is poured forth upon us; and the sanctification of men in Christ and the glorification of God, to which all other activities of the Church are directed as towards their end, is achieved in the most efficacious way possible.

11. . . . in order that the liturgy be able to produce its full effects, it is necessary that the faithful come to it with proper dispositions . . . Pastors of souls must therefore realize that, when the liturgy is celebrated . . . it is their duty . . . to ensure that the faithful take part fully aware of what they are doing, actively engaged in the rite . . .

14. . . . [The Church] earnestly desires that all the faithful should be led to that full, conscious, and active participation in liturgical celebrations which is demanded by the very nature of the liturgy. Such participation by the Christian people as a "chosen race, a royal priesthood, a holy nation, a redeemed people" (I Pet 2:9; 2:4-5), is their right and duty by reason of their baptism.

In the restoration and promotion of the sacred liturgy, this full and active participation by all the people is the aim to be considered before all else; for it is the primary and indispensable source from which the faithful are to derive the true Christian spirit. . . .[6]

---

[6] This section of the *Constitution* concludes with the admonition of the Council Fathers that priests and pastors be trained in the spirit and power of the liturgy. To this end professors of liturgy are to be thoroughly grounded in the science and history of liturgy. Liturgy is to be upgraded to a major discipline in seminaries and is to be taught under its theological, historical, and pastoral aspects. All other disciplines are to relate their material to the liturgical life of the Church. The spiritual training of seminarians is to be rooted in the liturgy.

C. *Actual Reform of the Sacred Liturgy:*

In order that the Christian people may more certainly derive an abundance of graces from the sacred liturgy, holy Mother Church desires to undertake with great care a general restoration of the liturgy itself. For the liturgy is made up of immutable elements divinely instituted, and of elements subject to change. These not only may but ought to be changed with the passage of time if they have suffered from the intrusion of anything out of harmony with the inner nature of the liturgy . . .

In this restoration, both texts and rites should be drawn up so that they express more clearly the holy things which they signify; the Christian people, so far as possible, should be enabled to understand them with ease and to take part in them fully . . .

(a.) General Norms:

23. That sound tradition may be retained, and yet the way remain open to legitimate progress, a careful investigation is always to be made into each part of the liturgy which is to be revised. This investigation should be theological, historical, and pastoral. . . .

(b.) Norms drawn from the Assembly Nature of the Liturgy:

26. Liturgical services are not private functions but are celebrations of the Church, which is the "sacrament of unity" . . .

. . . liturgical services pertain to the whole body of the Church; they manifest it and have effects upon it; but they concern the individual members of the Church in different ways, according to their differing rank, office, and actual participation.

30. To promote active participation, the people should be encouraged to take part by means of acclamations, responses, psalmody, antiphons, and songs, as well as by actions, gestures, and bodily attitudes.

(c.) Norms based on the Instructive, Pastoral Nature of the Liturgy:

33. Although the sacred liturgy is above all things the worship of the divine Majesty, it likewise contains much instruction for the faithful. For in the liturgy God speaks to his people and Christ is still proclaiming his gospel. . . .

Moreover, the prayers addressed to God by the priest who presides over the assembly in the person of Christ are said in the name of the entire holy people and of all present. And the visible signs used by the liturgy to signify invisible divine things have been chosen by Christ or the Church. Thus not only when things are read "which were written for our instruction" (Rom 15:4), but also when the Church prays and sings, or acts, the faith of those taking part is nourished and their minds are raised to God, so that they may offer him their rational service and more abundantly receive his grace.

[To this end] 34. The rites should be distinguished by a noble simplicity; they should be short, clear, and unencumbered by useless repetitions; they should be within the people's powers of comprehension . . .

35. That the intimate connection between words and rites may be apparent in the liturgy:

(i.) In sacred celebrations there is to be more reading from holy scripture, and it is to be more varied and suitable.

(ii.) Because the sermon is part of the liturgical service . . . the ministry of preaching is to be fulfilled with exactitude and fidelity. The sermon, however, should draw its content mainly from scriptural and liturgical sources, and its character should be that of a proclamation of God's wonderful works in the history of salvation, the mystery of Christ, ever made present and active within us, especially in the celebration of the liturgy.[7]

(iv.) Bible services should be encouraged, especially on the vigils of the more solemn feasts, on some weekdays in Advent and Lent, and on Sundays and feast days. . . .

36. . . . the use of the mother tongue, whether in the Mass, the administration of the sacrament, or other parts of the liturgy . . . may be extended.

Chapter II. The Sacred Mystery of the Eucharist [the *Constitution* now applies the general principles of reform to the Eucharist]:

47. At the Last Supper, on the night when he was betrayed, our Savior instituted the eucharistic sacrifice of his body and blood. He did this in order to perpetuate the sacrifice of the Cross throughout the centuries until he should come again, and so to entrust to his . . . Church a memorial of his death and

---

[7] In this connection: Art. 24 of the General Norms: "Sacred Scripture is of the greatest importance in the celebration of the liturgy. . . . to achieve the restoration, progress, and adaptation of the sacred liturgy, it is essential to promote that warm and living love for scripture to which the venerable tradition of both eastern and western rites gives testimony."

resurrection: a sacrament of love, a sign of unity, a bond of charity, a paschal banquet in which Christ is eaten, the mind is filled with grace, and a pledge of future glory is given to us.

48. The Church, therefore, earnestly desires that Christ's faithful, when present at this mystery of faith, should not be there as strangers or silent spectators; on the contrary, through a good understanding of the rites and prayers they should take part in the sacred action conscious of what they are doing, with devotion and full collaboration. They should be instructed by God's word and be nourished at the table of the Lord's body; they should give thanks to God; by offering the immaculate victim, not only through the hands of the priest, but also with him . . .

49. For this reason the Sacred Council . . . has made the following decress in order that the sacrifice of the Mass . . . may become pastorally efficacious to the fullest degree.

50. The rite of the Mass is to be revised in such a way that the intrinsic nature and purpose of its several parts . . . be more clearly manifested, and that devout and active participation by the faithful may be more easily achieved.

For this purpose the rites are to be simplified, due care being taken to preserve their substance; elements which, with the passage of time, came to be duplicated, or were added with but little advantage, are now to be discarded; other elements which have suffered injury through accidents of history are now to be restored . . .

51. The treasures of the Bible are to be opened up more lavishly, so that richer fare may be provided for the faithful at the table of God's word . . . .

52. By means of the homily, the mysteries of the faith and the guiding principles of the Christian life are expounded from the sacred text, during the course of the liturgical year; the homily, therefore, is to be highly esteemed as part of the liturgy . . .

53. . . . on Sundays and feasts of obligation there is to be restored, after the Gospel and the homily, "the common prayer" or "the prayer of the faithful."

54. In Masses which are celebrated with the people, a suitable place may be allotted to their mother tongue. . . .

. . . wherever a more extended use of the mother tongue within the Mass appears desirable, the regulation laid down in Art. 40 of this Constitution is to be observed. [re: missionary lands, etc.][8]

55. That more perfect form of participation in the Mass whereby the faithful, after the priest's communion, receive the Lord's body from the same sacrifice, is strongly commended.

. . . communion under both kinds may be granted when the bishops think fit, not only to clerics and religious, but also to the laity . . .

56. The two parts which, in a certain sense, go to make up the Mass, namely, the liturgy of the word and the eucharistic liturgy, are so closely connected with each other that they form but one single act of worship. Accordingly this sacred Synod strongly urges pastors of souls that, when instructing the faithful, they insistently teach them to take their part in the entire Mass . . .[9]

The spirit of this *Constitution* has already been translated into striking liturgical reform. Revisions in the official worship of the Church have been undertaken by the Vatican Liturgy Commission set up by Pope Paul VI; the first recommendations of this body, issued in the form of an instruction, are now being put into effect. Remarkable as these revisions are, they must be regarded as only a first step in a more comprehensive liturgical renewal that will be undertaken by this same Commission over the next several years. The initial changes, then, are transitional and are concerned with pointing up the community nature of Christian worship; they seek to increase the understanding, faith, and participation of the people. To this end they allow a great increase of the vernacular in the Mass and call for the active involvement of all the faithful. The major changes[10] as they apply to the Latin Mass are briefly as follows.

---

[8] Hopefully, liturgists believe this will open more vernacular for solidly Christian lands as well.

[9] Beyond the recommendations and decrees of the Two Chapters above, the *Constitution* continues its renewal of the liturgical life of the Church with chapters on "The Sacraments and Sacramentals"; "The Divine Office"; "The Liturgical Year"; "Sacred Music"; and "Sacred Art and Sacred Furnishing."

[10] First changes were put into effect in the United States at the end of 1964; these were supplemented by further changes which became effective at the start of the Lenten season, 1965.

Recent Revisions

The beginning and end of the rite have been simplified. Psalm 42 has been eliminated from the preparatory prayers said at the foot of the altar. The last Gospel and the prayers after Mass are also discontinued; the rite now ends with the final Blessing. These omissions are not meant to shorten the Mass; they will, however, allow more time to be given to the preaching of the Word, which the Council has insisted is an integral and important part of Christian worship.

The revised liturgy has reinstated the ancient "Prayer of the Faithful." This prayer is a brief series of invocations or petitions, mostly of an immediate and practical nature; it is said or sung at the completion of the Office of the Word (readings, homily, Creed). Three other prayers of the Mass have received the pastoral attention of the Liturgy Commission. These were among the most solemn and public prayers of the Mass, but for centuries they had been recited quietly by the priest. Now they are said or sung audibly so that all can hear and respond to them. They are: the prayer over the offerings, called the Secret prayer, which completes the preparation of the bread and wine; the Doxology prayer which concludes the Canon; and the prayer for deliverance from evil and for peace which follows the Lord's Prayer.

Of the "public" prayers of the Mass which the whole congregation should read and follow, only the body of the Canon (which still awaits revision) is presently said in a quiet voice and in Latin. But the instruction states that the priest is no longer to recite quietly or privately prayers which other ministers, the people, or the choir read or sing as their distinctive parts in the Mass. Duplications are thus eliminated. In the past, the priest also recited the parts of others, as, for example, the *Gloria,* even when this hymn was sung by the people. Obviously no intention is made here to unburden the priest of his duties. It is intended to make clear the community of roles in the liturgy, with each participant—priest, minister, and layman—offering his vital part to the common action of the Mass.

The reform-instruction recommends that in the Fore Mass it is preferable that the lector, whether cleric or layman, read the Epistle while the celebrant listens. The same lector may read the chants which follow the Epistle unless these are sung or recited by others. The Gospel reading is reserved (at solemn Mass) for the deacon or (at low Mass) for the celebrant. And even at low Mass the celebrant during the Office of the Word is allowed to remain apart from the altar (at *sedilia,* lectern, or pulpit); thus as presiding officer over the readings he draws attention to the importance and sacredness of the proclamation of the Word. The recitations are now in the vernacular and are rendered facing the people.

Normally the celebrant reserves his activity at the altar for the celebration of the Eucharist itself, beginning with the Offertory. To promote a sense of participation in the Office of the Eucharist and to show that the Mass is a sacrificial meal, the instruction allows and prefers (but does not require) that the altars be arranged for Mass with the celebrant facing the people. The renewed form of the Mass presently follows this order:

Office of the Word

PRAYERS AT THE FOOT OF THE ALTAR—"Introibo ad altare . . ."—LATIN (*Without Psalm 42*)
INTROIT—ENGLISH
KYRIE—"Lord have mercy . . ."—ENGLISH (*Priest and people alternating*)
GLORIA—"Glory to God in the highest . . ."—ENGLISH (*Priest and people together*)
COLLECT—LATIN[11]
EPISTLE—ENGLISH (*Facing the people*)
GRADUAL—ENGLISH
GOSPEL—ENGLISH (*Facing the people*)
HOMILY—ENGLISH
CREED—"I believe in one God . . ."—ENGLISH (*Priest and people together*)
PRAYER OF THE FAITHFUL—ENGLISH

[11] It seems likely that this prayer will soon be in English also.

Office of the Eucharist

OFFERTORY ANTIPHON—ENGLISH
SECRET PRAYER—LATIN[12] (*Recited audibly*)
PREFACE—"Vere Dignum et Justum est . . ."—LATIN
SANCTUS—"Holy, holy, holy . . ."—ENGLISH (*Priest and people together*)
THE REMAINDER OF THE CANON—LATIN (*Doxology conclusion recited audibly*)
THE LORD'S PRAYER—ENGLISH (*Priest and people together*)
AGNUS DEI—"Lamb of God . . ."—ENGLISH (*Priest and people together*)
OTHER PRAYERS PRECEDING THE PRIEST'S COMMUNION—LATIN
ECCE AGNUS DEI—"Behold the Lamb of God . . ."—ENGLISH
DOMINE, NON SUM DIGNUS—"Lord, I am not worthy . . ."—ENGLISH (*Priest and people together*)
COMMUNION ANTIPHON—ENGLISH
POST COMMUNION[12]—LATIN
DISMISSAL AND FINAL BLESSING—ENGLISH

Our day has thus seen a fruitful conclusion to the efforts of the great reforming liturgists and popes. And yet with so much reform in the air it is obvious that the ordinary Catholic has not yet been imbued with all the principles of liturgical renewal. The Church has much work before her to preach and teach the doctrinal reasons that motivate liturgical reform; the task of changing the mentality of the faithful so that they can profit fully from these changes is not one that will be easily discharged.

But the serious Catholic is gradually beginning to see that the liturgy of the Mass is not incidental to his faith, but the key action of his life. He is beginning to see himself and his brothers as a living Mystical Body, a worshiping assembly formed by Christ and in Christ to give true and perfect praise to the Father in whose glory we find the graces that make our life Christian. As he worships God in truth and in spirit with his brothers, enriched by his community prayer and grace-life, the Catholic feels better able to carry on his Christian commitment in the world. And as he becomes more conscious of his oneness with his Catholic brothers in

[12] It seems likely that these prayers also will soon be in English.

Christ, he is disturbed by his lack of full union with his separated brothers. And thus not the least of the blessings of the liturgical renewal has been a new awareness among Catholics of the need to pray and work for Christian unity. Visible unity at pulpit, altar, and rail is not viewed as some far off dream; it is seen as God's will, his commandment for us. We can not be indifferent to God's desires; we must work seriously to fulfill them.

Part Two

The Liturgy and Christian Unity

Chapter Four

Protestant Liturgy: An Ecumenical Appraisal

The liturgical and biblical renewals have done much to quicken within Christianity a genuine ecumenical spirit. Graces have been engendered among us which are moving the churches to a united community of faith and worship. We have gone our separate ways too long and sense more than ever the scandal of our divisions. If nothing else, our renewed liturgical and biblical life has taught us that the Kingdom of God is not to be confined to the private world of the individual. With earlier Christians we are beginning to see it again as a corporate Kingdom in whose communal faith, Sacraments, and worship, salvation is found for all men; we must work together to make the Christian Church a united visible "sign" before the nations (Isa 11:12), who, confronting it, will be convinced at last that Christ's mission is from the Father (Jo 17:21).

Non-Catholics rejoice that these renewals have prompted Catholics to stress less strongly the peripheral elements of the faith which tend to divide them from other Christians. The Catholic Church indeed is giving solid attention to the fundamentals of the Christian mystery, and such attention has made the Church more attractive and understandable to our separated brothers. The advances in friendship and mutual discussion of past years bear this out.

The Catholic Church is beginning to appear to the outsider less a society intent on defending its hierarchical structure and juridical power. Serious students of the Church see it proclaiming itself (and acting more like) God's worshiping community, which it believes itself to be. Before all else the Christian Church is Christ, living on in his priestly, Mystical Body. By our Baptism and continuing eucharistic life we live within the Body of the Mystical Christ and he within us; as members of our Lord we understand and take part in the fulfillment of his basic mission: the re-establishment of all creation in the redeeming worship of the Father.

The emphasis may seem new to some inside as well as outside the Church, since the "hierarchical-juridical" image was stressed so long, owing to the Reformation controversies which denied the societal structure of the Church. Still, this "new" image of the Church is a traditional pre-Tridentine one and our Orthodox and Protestant brothers find it extremely compatible with their own views. The image does not remove the doctrinal and juridical problems that separate us, but it provides a much more congenial climate in which to work toward the fulfillment of our ecumenical hopes.

This more dynamic view of the Church as Mystical Body, as Christ incarnate in the present generation has given rise to a sacramental theology that Protestants (as well as our own people) find much more understandable and meaningful. Christ, our one only mediator, is the primal Sacrament. Through the sign of his visible humanity he showed us the divinity and offered for us and as one of us the priestly oblation which reconciled us to God. Now his priestly work is carried on through the worshiping life of the Mystical Body. Christ perpetuates his saving work by means of his preached Word and enacted Sacraments. As he operated among us through the sacrament of his humanity, historically preaching, healing, cleansing, saving, so now he operates through his Mystical Sacrament, the Church. The preached Word and the enacted Sacraments (especially Baptism and the Lord's Supper) make the Incarnation a present reality until the end of time. It is not Peter or Paul who preaches, baptizes, and celebrates the Eucharist, but the Incarnate, Mystical Christ. His hand is still at work; his voice preaching, his lips praying. Whatever was externally salvific in his life is now contained in his visible Sacraments. Thus Sacraments, as continuing grace-filled "faith-encounters" within Christ (an insight that these recent renewals have recovered for us), provide us with a sacramental theology that serves ecumenism well; much better than the overweighted *ex opere operato* handling that stressed so little the responsive "faith-encounter" necessary to make Sacraments fully fruitful instruments of growing in the Christ-life.

The liturgical renewal has also restored the layman to his rightful place in the Church. He is no longer in any sense a second-class citizen. In his very being he is the Church; as Peter says, he belongs to the "royal priesthood" (I Pet 2:9), his Baptism consecrates him for worship. Worship is not a clerical preserve but the work and privilege of all the community who live within Christ. The restoration of a full integral role to the layman has received an extremely sympathetic reaction from the Protestant community. In fact, from them and Orthodox Christians we have much to learn. The lay responsibility which they have always respected and built into their church life should be studied by us as a model and goal toward our own full recognition of the laity.

The liturgical renewal then has given new dynamism to the ecclesiological and sacramental life of Catholics. The present effects of liturgical renewal on Protestant and Catholic worship have been noted. But this renewal has by no means fully penetrated the general stream of Protestant worship. Mr. Marshall has given us a good picture of this worship. We find that the ecumenical spirit is well served in many particulars, but, in our view, we also discover elements that tend to weaken this spirit. At this point it might be good to exchange critical views of our liturgies. We do this only to show what aspects of the worship of our separated brothers seem to us to promote or hinder the ecumenical spirit. There is much undoubtedly that we can learn from each other positively and negatively.

Worship in Fellowship

A Catholic looking in on Protestant worship[1] discovers there real Fellowship and Community. The Protestant congregation is one where the members usually know each other; the minister and the congregation are generally on speaking terms. There is a feeling of brotherhood in a common action of praise and thanksgiving, a sense of mutual discipleship in the witness of Christ. The elements that assist this community spirit are many. Obviously the use of the vernacular is responsible for intelligent participation. Protestants worship in their own language and so are able to understand and follow the service with ease. And the readings, prayers, hymns, and responses, usually cast in a good literary vernacular, are spoken, read, and sung in a reverent and prayerful way. The Catholic, in fact, is impressed at the "art" that Protestants show in the matter of saying their prayers reverently (the Catholic has a tendency to recite his prayers too fast and by rote).

Granting that there were periods in the evolution of Protestant worship that understressed it, Protestants have emphasized strongly the priesthood of all believers and have insisted that participation, involvement by all the members of the community, is an essential mark of worship. The family nature of the Christian flock is given expression when the "we" of the service is spoken by all the faithful.

The Catholic at Mass on the other hand can be overly concerned with himself, his worship obligations, his personal advancement in the Christ-life. The "super" reverence that has surrounded the Mass, the church building, the tabernacle, although it is extremely productive of the essential note of "Christ present" sometimes creates an exclusivist attitude of being "alone before Christ" and not of being "together with the brethren in Christ" (the aspect

---

[1] The author in his criticism draws not only from Mr. Marshall's enlightening presentation, but also from his own personal observations of Protestant worship over a ten-year period.

that should characterize Mystical Body worship). Some feel that acknowledging the presence of their fellow Christians is something of a distraction, almost to be discouraged. It would seem that a blend of reverence and open community could well be more in evidence at Catholic Mass. If we believe strongly that we are a community (and we must), then there should be more external, friendly acknowledgment of this belief. Obviously the reforms of the Second Vatican Council allowing an increase in community action will help to create an atmosphere of open fellowship at Mass.

If the Catholic can volunteer any criticism here, it would be more in the nature of degree than of kind. He is greatly impressed when he finds community among Protestants. He is only disturbed when he discovers that the community, though real, is not as theologically grounded as he feels it should be. The worship is indeed communal, but the faith of the community is sometimes highly personalized and fragmented. The Catholic sees the Church not as an aggregate of private believers but as a community of common believers who witness in mutual faith the full Christian mystery. Community worship to be truly *ecumenical,* he feels, must well from a *united* community of faith.

Also, the Catholic is uneasy when he discovers a sense of *ad libitum* in the matter of worship attendance. It is true that Protestants want to worship only with a "willing community"; this is good. But again the Catholic thinks that the Church as a whole must be projected and viewed always as a worshiping assembly; it may be other things but it is essentially this. Therefore we must stress the obligations that our Baptism imposes on all of us to live our priestly consecration by joining our brothers in the Lord for the saving praise of the Father. Community is community. We cannot say we are formed to worship in community and then be less than serious about our community obligations. Certainly it is necessary to stress personal will and commitment, but to embrace Christianity only as an individual or "occasional" covenant, with no respect for corporate benefit and corporate responsibilities, the Catholic feels, is to compromise the Church as Mystical Body. Our greatest Christian act, our most grace-filled act, is that in which we join our brothers in Christ in the visible worship of our loving

Father. The Catholic feels a sense of sadness about a service which even tacitly admits that what is going on in community worship could just as well be done singly by Christians off by themselves.

Flexibility

When one studies the liturgy under the guidance of Mr. Marshall he comes to realize that Protestants as a group have been more sensitive to the changing temper of the faithful. And thus Protestant worship has shown a flexibility and adaptability that usually is slow in coming to Catholic liturgy. There is surely an objectivity, an essential shape to the liturgy that comes from God and with which we are not at liberty to tamper (and which authority must protect). Still the given reality of worship must be adjusted to the civilizations, customs, problems of the "contemporary Christian," and by and large Protestants have been quicker than Catholics to adjust worship to meet the needs of the faithful and to make worship meaningful for people in their particular stage of advancement in the Christian commitment.

High Respect for the Word

The Catholic is deeply moved by the importance Protestants give to the proclamation of the Word. They obviously look upon the Book as God's greatest gift to the Church; if another precious gift, the Eucharist, seems to be understressed in worship, at least our liturgies coincide in their mutual reverence for Scripture. Protestants and Catholics join each other in believing that the Word becomes active in worship; the Bible is no longer simply an apologetical source book, a recorded chronicle of static events in salvation history. When the minister preaches Scripture, it becomes a "living Word." "For the word of God is living and efficient and keener than any two-edged sword . . . extending even to the division of soul and spirit . . . a discerner of the thoughts and intentions of the heart." (Heb 4:12) "Is not my word like fire, says the Lord, like a hammer shattering rocks?" (Jer 23:29) The Gospel catches us up in that perfect dialogue between God and his people which was established by Christ in whom we know, hear, and speak to the Father. In the Word, Jesus as man speaks for us to the Father; as the Word of God he is the epitome of the Father's will for us. The preached Word lives; it is addressed to us and demands our response here and now. As Jesus asks his disciples: "Who do men say that I am?" the Gospel moves us to answer with Peter: "You are the Christ, the son of the living God!" The whole Gospel account of Christ: his miracles, his commandment sermons, his didactic discourses and parables, the creation of his sacramental gifts—challenge our response, and so often that response has been formed for us in the inspired words of Scripture itself: the Our Father, the Psalms, the Canticles, the many "faith responses" of Christ's first followers: "I do believe, help my unbelief"—"You alone have the words of eternal life"—"Truly this was the son of God"—"My Lord and my God!" Protestants by centering their liturgy in the saving Word are drawn toward Christ as Lord and Savior and are able to make worship a living response of faith.

Catholics can have no issue with their separated brothers in giving so high a place to the Word; if anything they can learn a lesson in proper emphasis. Catholics must be on the alert never to sacrifice the primacy of the Word in the Fore Mass. Though it is there, its primacy has sometimes been hard to discern amid the embellishments. We are thankful that the Second Vatican Council has called for a clear and unmistakable primacy of position to be given to the Word. And with the advent of more and more vernacular in worship it is to be hoped that Catholics will become as scripturally well versed as Protestants. Scripture is a living Word; it is imperative that Catholics hear, sing, and pray more of it—their devotional and prayer life should be sustained and nourished by it, as is the case with most Protestants.

If the Catholic feels that any criticism is in order, it is in the use he sometimes finds Scripture put to. If the Word were used primarily as proclamation, here and now involvement in a living and saving dialogue to which we were to respond in faith and action, there would be little cause for critical comment. It seems to many Catholics, however, that the Word is used by Protestants all too often (and by Catholics often enough) simply as a referral source for moral commandments. Morality is essential to the Christian life. But Christianity is concerned also with unity, mystery, saving dialogue, Sacraments, divine indwelling, oneness with Father, Son, and Spirit, etc. So seldom do we hear of the great mysteries from which must flow our moral commitment. The Word should proclaim these saving truths; this is what the Catholic means when he calls for "biblical preaching." If special conduct is required of the Christian, if unity is a task imperative on all of us, it is because of what we are and of what we can become, of the special vocation and powers that have been given us.

Lack of the Peripheral

Another commendable aspect of Protestant worship (and a great help to ecumenism) is its lack of the peripheral. Centered around Christ as Lord and Savior the service proceeds along simple, uncluttered lines. It is directed to the Father, but all proceeds clearly through Christ, our one only mediator. Catholics have much to learn here. Their rite, though intrinsically Christo-centric, has become overloaded, as we have seen. In its elaborateness, the simple structure of the liturgy as saving Word and unifying, sanctifying Sacrament has not always been clearly defined. The Council has called for a restoration of simplicity and clarity in this regard and recent enactments have gone a long way toward a clearer definition of the rite. Further suitable reforms will be suggested in the following chapter.

Protestant liturgies in their Christo-centric direction need no improvement. Still the Catholic feels that Protestant worship could more strongly project a spirit of the *presence* of Christ. Our Lord's Incarnational extension in time through his mystical indwelling in Christians (though taught) is not always sensed. As we will see, Christ's Sacramental oneness with us is not fully appreciated by Protestants. One would like to see the indwelling of Christ stressed more, an indwelling that is especially manifest at worship when the community formed in him carries out its highest act. Loyalty, fidelity, allegiance, responsiveness: these are all necessary in the Christian commitment, but too often the obligations that follow from commitment will be forgotten unless we realize, particularly in the sacred action of worship, that we are in truth indwelt by

Christ as are all our brothers. Christ is not only transcendent Lord, teaching us the truths that lead to heaven. He has never left us and is within the Body of the Church forming us more solidly into a community of grace and faith.

Also, Catholics (though admitting that the peripheral must give way to the essential) are sometimes a little startled at the "super" simplicity they find in Protestant worship. The Catholic liturgist believes that worship should be simple, but this is not to mean that it should exclude human, symbolic elements. The Catholic worships God not only in spirit but in body and sense; he feels that there is a need for visible signs, meaningful gestures, bodily involvement. Worship that downplays symbolism seems to him inhuman, and to deny that we are body as well as spirit, and that Christ has pledged a share in his glory to both.

Sacramental Renewal

Perhaps the most ecumenically hopeful aspect the Catholic sees in Protestant worship is the restoration in some churches of Holy Communion as an integral part of the service. Protestants find that our biblical renewal has brought us much closer to them; in like manner Catholics view the Protestant sacramental renewal as a great source of ecumenical hope. From what has been said it must be easier for Protestants to understand why Catholics attach such importance to eucharistic worship. And Mr. Marshall has shown that Protestants in "rediscovering" the Eucharist are not innovating or imitating, but returning to what the great reformers insisted was an essential part of worship; worship that contained a balanced use of Word and Sacrament had the most meaning for Calvin, Luther, and the Wesleys. The Eucharist is our Bread and Meal of unity, the sacred grains of wheat which form us into the one bread of Christ, the sign to ourselves and the world that we are one in Christ. "For we being many are one bread, one body, all that partake of the one bread." (I Cor 10:17) If we are to live and act as one, then Christ must solidify and protect that unity in grace. Catholics rejoice that Protestants join them in the belief that this is done in the renewal of the Lord's Supper. Our Lord tells us: "He who eats my flesh and drinks my blood is united with me and

I with him." (Jo 6:56) Baptism is but the first step in our unity within the Lord; unity must grow and be solidified through the Eucharist where Christ builds to fullness our oneness with him and the brethren. In our eucharistic life we realize that we are a family, a community, that we constitute a Mystical Body whose unity can only be nourished by the Eucharistic Body of Christ. Christian unity, then, is pre-eminently a sacramental matter for Catholics. St. Cyril of Alexandria gives eloquent expression to this theological position:

> To merge us in unity with God and among ourselves, although we have each a distinct personality, the only Son devised a wonderful means: through one only body, his own, he sanctifies his faithful in mystic communion, making them one body with him and among themselves. Within Christ no division can arise. All united to the single Christ through his own body, all receiving him, the one and indivisible, into our own bodies, we are the members of this one body and he is thus, for us the bond of unity.[2]
>
> . . . divided as it were into distinct personalities by which one is Peter or John or Thomas or Matthew, we are, so to speak, molded into one sole body in Christ feeding on one flesh alone. One spirit singles us out for unity, and as Christ is one and indivisible, we are all no more but one in him. So did he say to his heavenly Father, "That they may be one, as we are one."[3]

In community Communion we discover who we are, and by the grace of the Eucharistic Christ, we become more of what we are, the very Body of Christ. And the Catholic cannot reserve the role of teacher to himself. He can learn as he observes Protestant eucharistic practice. When Protestants celebrate the Sacrament, the fellowship, community meal is more clearly defined than in his own rite. This is fostered by sharing in the sacred cup as well as the bread. As the congregation eats and drinks *together* one senses that along with personal nourishment, the meal, as with all family meals, is working community edification.

If the Catholic has reservations about the Protestant sacramental renewal, it is in the fact that sometimes he finds a lack of theo-

---

[2] *In Joannem,* 11, 11 P.G., lxxiv, 560.

[3] *De Trinitate,* P.G., lxxv, 695.

logical substance behind the use of the Lord's Supper. Some celebrate the Eucharist as *mere* sign, and as mere symbol the Sacrament can have little effective, unifying force. Unity is from Christ and is advanced by intensification of our common life within him. Symbols and signs alone can not bring this about; only Christ effectively present in his signs can make us one. Eucharistic practice which denies a real operative presence of Christ can hardly inspire an awareness of our mystical unity in him. Eucharistic worship is unitive worship. The Catholic feels that the history of the Church is eloquent to show that Christians have believed that Eucharistic Communion is the Sacrament of Christ's presence, given as the invitation to and the formative instrument of union with himself and the brethren.

The Catholic of course deeply regrets that sacramental renewal has not influenced the mainstream of Protestant worship as yet. Christian unity as we have said is worked by Christ. In the Catholic view his unitive instruments are especially the Word and the Lord's Supper. Our unitive edification needs the proclamation of the Word that we might be united in mind with Christ; but it also needs the partaking of the Eucharist that we might become one body and spirit with him.

Architectural Revival

Catholics view with approval the architectural revival within Protestantism. Many new temples of worship show a strong ecumenical inspiration in design. Churches are getting away from the town meeting appearance and are being built in a way that indicates the family, priestly structure of believers (circular, semicircular in shape, more intimate arrangement of pews in reference to altar, pulpit, etc.). Many churches have restored the altar as a point of focus. The pulpit and the altar are given arresting and balanced positions; people thus see that worship is polarized around Word and Sacrament.

In the new churches Protestants give an important position to the baptismal font. As the place of liturgical birth it is situated in a striking place, usually close to altar and pulpit. Some Protestants have even called for the removal of the lectern and a placing of the font in its stead.[4] Catholics can take a lesson here. So often they put the baptismal font in the drabbest, least visible place in the church. If Baptism forms us for worship by incorporating us into our worshiping Lord, it should be given a striking position where its relationship to altar and pulpit is clearly defined. Certainly as both of us grow in awareness that Baptism is a new birth into the community of the worshiping Christ, we will more likely respect our obligations and participate more actively in worship.

[4] S. F. Brenner, *The Art of Worship* (New York: The Macmillan Company, 1961), p. 13.

Chapter Five

Catholic Liturgy: An Ecumenical Introspection

The recent early reforms prompted by *The Constitution on the Sacred Liturgy* have already made the Catholic Mass a more understandable and inspiring rite for our people; its form has certainly become more meaningful to our separated brethren. Thus these changes have already served the ecumenical cause well. But the changes are admittedly just a start, transitional reforms on the way to the fuller reformation called for in the *Constitution*. A liturgical commission has been charged by the Pope with the task of formulating these fuller and more comprehensive revisions. In light of the fact, therefore, that present changes in the Mass are only a welcome beginning, we might review some of the suggestions that liturgists propose as desirable if the rite is to assist the move toward Christian unity.

Liturgy a Prayer for Unity

Our worship in Christ is a prayer of adoration and thanksgiving to God as creator, sustainer, and giver of the new life. It is also a petition for the present needs of the Church. No greater need confronts the Christian Church than outward unity, a unity that will remove the scandal of fragmentation and show the world that Christ is mystically present and still Lord of the universe, a unity that will serve as his designated sign to the nations of the divine validity of his message (Jo 17:11). The Mass, as the Catholic's prayer of petition, must always seek stronger bonds of unity among Catholics and with those who do not share full faith and order with them. Catholics, believing the Church is already one and indefectible in nature, generally are not sufficiently disturbed by the scandal of a divided Christendom. They must be taught to see that the Church's essential unity is not yet fully realized in all particulars and in all Christians; full unity is now frustrated by the compromises, schisms and sins of Christians—Catholic, Orthodox, and Protestant. Therefore we must pray to make unity fully effective. In the Prayer of the Faithful, now revived, Catholics have a powerful supplicative moment in which to petition unity. They should pray fervently in every Mass for Christian unity, and in the prayer express contrition for their part in the separation of Christians.[1] Repeating Christ's unity prayer, they should entreat the Father to hasten the day when our Lord's prayer will be fulfilled in outward manifestation and there will be "one flock and one shepherd." Unity thus would be before them as a *need* and they would be taking the most salutary step to answer the need—community prayer and confession.

[1] The Prayer of the Faithful should allow for silent moments of prayer so that individuals can recall with repentance their own personal sins that have contributed to Christian fragmentation. Who can doubt that having said such a prayer, our relations with our fellow Christians would show more genuine fraternity?

Unqualified Primacy for the Word in the Fore Mass

The Constitution on the Sacred Liturgy insists that the Word be given a predominant place in worship. The biblical revival has shown that much of the Sacred Word originated as an expression of the worship life of the early Church. If much of Scripture was the Church's original worship dialogue with God it should be no less conspicuous in our modern Mass. The liturgy of the Word must be celebrated incisively and indicate that God speaks and sanctifies us in and through the holy proclamation. This will call for striking reformation of the Fore Mass. Along with the pruning of peripheral supports (elaborate *Kyries, Glorias,* etc.) there must be a better and more inclusive selection of Scripture readings so that the faithful hear and experience the full sweep of salvation history. The Word has sacramental force in the soul of the Christian when proclaimed; if so, our liturgy should show it sacramental reverence and attention. In Scripture we learn anew that God has not come to condemn the world but to transform it, to redeem and unite it within himself. The same power of love and obedience that effected Jesus' resurrection from the dead is ready to bestow new life on all who accept the Christ of Scripture. Hearing the Word we are able to penetrate deeply into the redemptive acts of God and see them as realized in the present moment. The Word is a living and saving Word; it must shine as a beacon through the Fore Mass and its spirit should follow through and be phrased into the whole rite. We, as Christ, are witnesses of the Father. What better way to speak our witness than in the inspired words of Christ and the prophets? Such clear and incisive biblical testimony will certainly draw us closer to our Protestant brothers whose witness has always been strongly biblical.

Simplicity and Flexibility

The *Constitution* states that the Mass is to be made simpler and more understandable. Liturgists speak with unanimity of the reforms that will effect simplicity and intelligibility. In their desire to see the Mass completely intelligible they stress that the entire rite must be in the language of the people and spoken in an audible tone that commands attention and permits intelligent participation. We are a community, our worship is the worship of the Mystical Body and it should have meaning for all of us and come from all of us; an audible vernacular is an absolute *sine qua non*. No effort must be spared to use the vernacular to cast the Mass in an evocative rite whose purpose comes through with solid impact. We come to Mass to love and praise our Father through union with Christ in Word and Sacrament. Anything that detracts from the central purpose of liturgy should be eliminated, e.g., any elaborate fussiness over vestments, pontifical gestures and incensings, rigid rubrical attitudes, repetitious chants and signs, and the use of symbols that have lost their meaning. What remains should not require extensive catechesis to explain its presence; if it has obvious meaning, it should stay, if it has lost its meaning, it should go.

In the effort to simplify the Mass, we should seriously consider the value of removing tabernacles from the altar to chapels of reservation. This would highlight the fact that the Mass is an exceedingly special coming, a special presence, a mystical unitive meal with Christ. Now the reserved presence seems to overshadow the Mass and render it in a way an action which is subordinate to our Lord's reserved presence.

But even in restoration the rite should not be rigidly "simple" but admit of flexibility and adaptability. In its simplicity the rite must be sensitive to adjust to the needs and temperament of the people. Its form is not to be determined by any absolutist view of what form should be, but allow for periodic modernizing of the rite as an effective prayer for contemporary Christians. Certainly as the rite projects a sacred simplicity, shows itself intelligible and flexible, our Protestant brothers will recognize more easily that we are a worshiping assembly whose main concern at Mass is to unite ourselves in Spirit with Christ in loving worship of the Father. We are not engaged in mystery rites or superstition. We are not doing things by rote without comprehension. Consciously and corporately we are all caught up in the action we were formed within Christ to perform. Such a rite, devoid of the peripheral and polemical, will render us more understandable and approachable;

and this cannot help but solicit the respect of Protestants and foster the ecumenical spirit.

Truly Corporate Worship

And as we work for intelligibility in expression we must stress constantly that our worship is community worship. Some Catholics show little urgency for Christian unity (i.e., restoration of full community) because they have fallen victim to the attitude of mind which sees the faith as an individual covenant, not one made individually within the redeemed community. Catholics often fail to realize that Christ's covenant is with his people, the New Israel, and individuals, so highly loved by him, are saved as they adhere to him within the redeemed community. Grace is not bestowed as a purely individual relationship between the soul and God; individuals receive grace in proportion as they are joined socially to the Messianic community where Christ preserves the graces of new life. Nowhere should this sense of salvation in community be more manifest than at Mass where the community performs its most distinctive act and declares most dramatically that it is the Mystical Body. If there is exaggerated individualism within the Church (and there is plenty of it) it is because the faithful have not been allowed (until recently) to participate actively in worship. Their community role has been confined too often to passive presence; if they reacted by taking refuge in individualistic devotions and prayers they cannot much be blamed. We are greatly thankful that the Council has called for a restoration of participation in the Mass and thus brought back to the Church a spirit of real community. The *Constitution* states: "Mother Church earnestly desires that all the faithful should be led to that full, conscious, and active participation in liturgical celebrations which is demanded by the very nature of liturgy. Such participation by the Christian people as a 'chosen race, a royal priesthood, a holy nation, a redeemed people' (I Pet 2:9; 2:4-5) is their right and duty by reason of their baptism." (Art. 14) Our Baptism gives us a personal vocation to worship. But our vocation is fulfilled in the community, in the hierarchically ordered assembly of the faithful where each has an integral role to play; our response is not that of a collection of individuals, but rather of a family of persons, a real worshiping community. And to deprive any Christian of his privilege of full participation with and in Christ at the communal Mass is not only to offend him in justice, in virtue of his priesthood; it is also to deny him an occasion for entering more deeply into the mystery of Christ and therefore a sin against charity. The priesthood of believers calls all Christians to listen to the Lord and to respond to him, to receive his gifts and to offer thanks in a truly priestly manner. The temptation to indulge in forms of clericalism, however subtle, must be totally rejected. The priesthood of the ordained minister must be seen as serving and promoting the universal priesthood, never as supplanting it or rendering it incidental. Participation then cannot help but quicken within the faithful a sense of their priestly unity; it will obviously quicken the desire to be more fully one with all who acknowledge Christ as Lord and Savior.

And within the community we need not fear that we will lose our individuality. We have our single problems, our single joys, all of which are extremely personal, and these are brought individually to Christ to be added to his offering. The rite therefore should allow for private prayer: moments of silent adoration, thanksgiving, and petition. The rite, primarily communal, must show that the community is not an impersonal abstraction, but a family of persons who have made personal as well as corporate covenant with Christ. In the company of our brothers, our personal spirits will be nourished; our sorrows sustained by the strength of the community and our joys in some measure redounding to the good of the whole community. Individuality expressed in this way will less likely degenerate into selfish individualism.

Eucharist as Sacrament of Unity[2]

The Mass rite must clearly identify the Eucharist as our great Sacrament of Christian unity. Certainly it is the Sacrament of "Christ-with-us," the Sacrament of presence and nourishment, the

[2] For a more extensive development of this concept, see Henri De Lubac, *Catholicism,* Part I, Chapter III (New York: Longmans, Green & Co., Inc., 1950), pp. 35-50.

eternal sacrifice rendered present in the world of contemporary Christianity. But it is also our great manifestation of unity in Christ and in each other and the source of intensifying that unity. Presently so few Catholics appreciate the unitive function of the Eucharist. If they associate unity with the Sacrament they consider it more personal than corporate. Still, Scripture and tradition have been eloquent to proclaim the unitive nature of the Lord's Supper. Paul's words are clear: "For we being many are one bread, one body, all that partake of the one bread" (I Cor 10:17). Trent is no less clear: "It was the will of Christ to make of this sacrament the symbol of that body of which he is himself the head, to which he would bind us as his members by the close bonds of faith, hope, and charity, so that all should be but one reality with never a division." [3] In earlier times Christians were very conscious of this aspect of the Eucharist. They saw an integral relationship between the mysteries of the *real presence* and the *Mystical Body*. An excerpt from St. Basil's liturgy shows how clearly the early Fathers saw the unitive causality of the Sacrament. At the consecration of the Mass the liturgy prayed that ". . . all of us who partake of this one bread and chalice be united to one another in the communion of the same Spirit." [4] This idea found its echo in an early Armenian liturgy: "We beseech thee, O Lord, send thy holy Spirit upon us and upon these present gifts so that, by sanctifying this bread and this chalice . . . he may make all of us who partake of this one bread and one chalice indissolubly one." [5] Another ancient liturgy in conjunction with the kiss of peace prayed: "O God of mercy and forbearance, we cry to thee in unison: Grant us that we may bestow peace upon each other in the holy kiss . . . make of us one holy people, save us by uniting us with one another, that we may sing thy praises. . . ." [6] With the evangelist John the early Church saw a clear connection between Christ's eucharistic discourse (Jo c. 6) and his prayer for unity (Jo c. 17). And it is in such a context: Christ's oneness with us in the Eucharist and his prayer for unity among his followers that the Catholic should

[3] Quoted in De Lubac, op. cit., p. 39.
[4] Ibid., p. 48.
[5] Quoted in *Oriens christianus,* Neue serie, vol. 3, 1913, p. 23.
[6] From St. Eustace, P.G., xviii, 697 and 698.

ground his devotion to this Sacrament. He does not fully understand the action of the "breaking of the bread" if he does not see it as the sign and source of fraternal communion. St. Fulgentius[7] puts this so eloquently:

> At no time may the spiritual building of the Body of Christ which charity effects, be implored more opportunely than when Christ's body, the Church, in the sacrament of the bread and of the chalice, offers the very Body and Blood of Christ. For "the chalice of benediction which we bless is it not the communion of the blood of Christ? And the bread which we break is it not the partaking of the body of the Lord? For we, being many, are one bread, one body: all that partake of the one bread." This is why we pray that by that same grace which has made the Church the body of Christ, all its members may persevere, held fast by the cement of charity in the unity of his body. . . .[8]

It would seem most desirable to return (more than occasionally) to reception of the Sacrament under the twofold signs of bread and wine. Our Lord gave us himself in the dual sign as the sacramental memorial of his last supper and saving death; he urged us to partake by eating *and* drinking. The Western Church, it is true, has a long custom of communicating under the sign of bread only. It would be necessary to give an extensive catechesis to our people to explain the symbolism of twofold communion. But the ancient custom is rich in meaning for Christian fellowship and would undoubtedly draw us closer to Eastern and Protestant Christians who have always communicated in this manner. The *Constitution* has urged this; liturgists only hope that a provocative rite for this form of communion will be devised and that pastors will take seriously the charge to use it.

Finally, the liturgical "dismissal" must clearly indicate that we who have proclaimed our unity in Christ are now clearly charged to go forth and express that unity in action. Having come in unity with our brothers, having grown in that unity through participation in Word and Sacrament we are to go into the world and com-

---

[7] A disciple of St. Augustine, he was bishop of Ruspe in North Africa and died in A.D. 533.

[8] *Ad Monimum,* Lib. II, c. xi, P.L., lxv, 190-91.

municate a real spirit of brotherhood toward our fellow Christians and to all men through charity, justice, zeal, and tolerance. The Christian is an individual, but he is not an individualist who cares little about his brothers or about those who could be his brothers. In his daily life he extends the unity and peace of Christ to others by his life of Christian witness. As Max Lackmann says in his theological explanation of the "dismissal" in the proposed *Evangelical Mass:*

> The community is sent into the world as "Christ bearers" "in the peace of the Lord," that they may light and serve the world as "the light of the world." . . . [protected by] . . . fellowship with the Triune God, the people of God must now return to the "worship of their daily lives" and glorify God by giving him their "living and dying," their victories and sufferings, and in this way celebrate the Eucharist of "living with God." [9]

---

[9] "The Evangelical Mass," *Yearbook of Liturgical Studies* (Notre Dame, Ind.: Fides Publishers, 1963), IV, 76.

Chapter Six

Liturgy and Christian Unity

The ecumenical spirit has dissipated much of the bitterness our fathers felt toward each other. Our relations, though not yet familial, are friendly. We talk in calmer tones with knowledge in mind not argument. But our links at present are almost exclusively conversational. The fact is that we do very little praying together. It would seem that now the ecumenical spirit needs more than all else the sustenance and enlightenment that comes from common prayer. Ecumenical effort that stops this side of prayer and worship is really only begun. Even our ecumenical discussions need a context of common prayer if they are to bear fruit. We must not only mutually search into the meaning of Scripture, we must hear and respond to the Word of God in community. A full union of faith and order is our goal, but that end is beyond our capacities to realize. But God has willed such unity, ecumenists believe, and he bids us to pray for it as he himself prayed to the Father that his apostles might be one as he and the Father were one (Jo 17:11).

Admitting that prayer is our most effective instrument to assist us in our advance toward Christian unity, can we come together in sincerity to pray for this great end? We can join with each other in informal prayer certainly; but can we worship together formally? Regretfully such worship presents many problems. Enthusiasts would like all restrictions set aside, urging Protestants to worship side by side with Catholics and vice versa; even to take the Holy Sacrament together. But this is to misunderstand the meaning and significance of formal worship as we have tried to outline it in the foregoing chapters. Intercommunion, which is what the enthusiasts are calling for, is for the Catholic (and I know that this is true for many Protestants) an extraordinary step and one that is nearer the climax of full union than a normal means of bringing us there. Why is this so?

Intercommunion

Common worship expresses a fullness of belief, i.e., in thought, sentiment, in the whole area of faith and ecclesiastical order. The sign and Sacrament of this fullness is especially the common sharing of Holy Communion. Participation in the Eucharist means for the responsible Catholic that he has been graced into the oneness of Christ and is united in supernatural union with his brothers; together they share a fullness of faith that encompasses every particular of the Creed. If they were in any way disjoined in faith by schism, heresy, or whatever, they would not be sacramentally proclaiming their unity in Christ. The Eucharist as sign and source of unity in faith and grace is the liturgy of ecumenical climax not the liturgy of ecumenical hope.

But some theologians, admitting that the Eucharistic liturgy is the sign and symbol of our unity in Christ, ask: Is not the Lord's Supper also given to us to effect this unity? This is true, and the

Catholic partakes of the Eucharist that he might grow in oneness with Christ and the brethren. It is conceivable then that in the matter of ecumenical prayer, intercommunion could be celebrated on rare and very special occasions for this purpose. But normally intercommunion is the desired end not the means of bringing us together in faith and worship. But if the prospects for formal intercommunion are remote, can we unite at prayer in other ways?

Another Form of Common Worship

Although Catholics have rigidly avoided worshiping with their separated brothers on the grounds that so doing has a tendency to promote indifferentism and to compromise the faith of Catholics (cf. Canon 1258, *Communicatio in sacris*), there is cause to believe that a day is coming when these restrictions will be relaxed, precisely because certain forms of common worship can be devised which will not compromise the faith of Protestants or Catholics. Remarkably there is emerging within the Catholic Church a "paraliturgical" service that greatly resembles the liturgy of the Word. It would seem that in the Catholic "Bible Vigil" and in the Protestant "Service of the Word" we have acceptable ground for common prayer. The "Bible Vigil," after all, is just a modern variation of the traditional Christian synaxis service which is mother to both Protestant Worship and the Catholic Fore Mass. It is true that the service is strongly instructional with its emphasis on Scripture and homily; some would say that it has a "catechumenal" quality. But though instruction predominates, there is also community response by means of hymns and prayers; it is therefore true Christian worship and an especially worthy form for divided Christians to use in their prayer for unity. In this service the one Christ proclaims the one Gospel to a flock divided but in search of unity. As we submit to the saving Word, Christ can make clear to us his plan of salvation. He can speak to us of the unity he wants for us, of the means we must use to effect it. He will show us the unity we already have, which, as further commitments are given, can issue in that greater oneness we know he wants for us. In a sense the service is suited for ecumenical "catechumens" who need a preparative novitiate before entering into the full Eucharistic life of the Church (which connotes wholeness of faith). The important thing is that we would be praying together, engaging our mightiest weapon in the campaign for Christian unity. Years may go by before such a common liturgy can be worked out. There is the problem of place, time, reciprocity, etc. But with patient effort an acceptable service can be devised which will proclaim before God the sincerity of our searching and give a telling example to all men that Christians, admitting their divisions, have come together to learn anew the demands of Christian unity and to beg from God the graces to accept and live those demands.

There is a great ecumenical value in working for a common service of the Word. The churches would finally have a common service of the baptized which would not proclaim full unity but petition it, asking for the graces necessary to illumine our minds and hearts. The service would remove the polemical overtones that have occasionally made our liturgies of the Word expressions of what we are against more than of what we are for. Its main thrust would be in stressing the elements that unite us, of educating us in the unitive fundamentals of the faith and of making us aware of the scandal of Christian fragmentation. Such prayer will surely undercut bigotry and misunderstanding and create a genuine feeling of brotherhood among us. If any reason has prolonged our divisions, it is this lack of a sense of true brotherhood; we considered each other less brothers than adherents of almost wholly different religions. We are brother Christians and in common prayer we will come to realize this.

In mutual prayer we will understand the corporate character of salvation. We will see that we are more than individuals before God; we are a family. He saved us as a family and he wants us as a "united people" to share our salvation with the world. Certainly our individuality will not be sacrificed in such a rite; it will be discovered all the more, because put in the context of family where we see that we have a stake in each other's happiness, heartaches, love, and glory. Most of all the world, seeing our community of prayer, will have cause for edification; the elements of scandal will be removed to a degree at least.

Common Rituals

Since the rite above would be comprised of Scripture, hymns, and prayers, there could develop in the Church (much more quickly than there is developing at present) a common Bible, Hymnal, and Book of Prayer. These in themselves would powerfully assist the ecumenical movement. Ecumenists can testify how different bibles magnify problems and tend to solidify our divisions; an interchurch service of the Word would greatly expedite the creation of a common bible. Many of our hymns and prayers are mutually acceptable; in fact, we have much to learn from each other in the way we pray and sing to God. Out of a unitive service of the Word could possibly emerge common baptismal, marriage, and funeral services which would show the world that Christians confront the critical moments of life with common faith and ritual.

Common prayer will not happen overnight. It is a great step, but one in view of Christ's command, that we must seriously consider. Christ urged his followers to guard their unity, to be vigilant and to pray. Our common prayer would be our "vigil," a most fitting one to use in the cause of Christian unity.

Periodic Intercommunion

After a history of common prayer, we would be better disposed to undertake occasional intercommunion together. Aware of our basic spiritual unity (despite our division), realizing also the operative power of Christ in the Sacrament of Union, we could approach the Eucharist not as a sign of union in faith and worship, but as an extraordinary supplication for God's intervention in our move toward unity. The whole rite therefore would be a "qualified" intercommunion, a prayer for union not a proclamation of union.[1]

[1] Some theologians state that theoretically intercommunion is possible with Orthodox Christians on a reciprocal basis, since Catholics recognize the validity of Orthodox priestly orders; this, however, would not be the case with Protestants and Anglicans. Even here in time it seems that intercommunion services (among Protestants and Anglicans who share belief in Christ's real unitive presence) could involve in their reciprocity our own priests and thus hurdle an obstacle which is admittedly a great one. At all

Unity is Christ's work; it calls for his extraordinary intervention. The greatest of his unitive works, we believe, is the Eucharist—the bread which declares and effects a miracle of unity when we partake of it with living faith. The day of supplicative intercommunion is obviously far off, but it can be set up as an ecumenical goal, a penultimate step in our journey toward full union.

Other Possibilities

Could there be other intermediate steps before intercommunion? Perhaps occasionally as separated brothers we could exchange pulpits (or lecterns if pulpits seem too sacrosanct) to speak and preach on the subject of Christian unity; some of this has already been done. There could be exchange groups to join in special prayers for Christian unity. As our liturgies experience the effects of renewal, there should be a removal of restrictions for the observation of the worship of our Protestant brothers and vice versa; both of us should allow participation for other Christians in limited ways (our liturgies should respect the faith of the observers and provide special times when participation could be given without compromise of faith).[2]

A very wonderful gesture (as suggested by Dr. Cullmann) would be the exchange of Offertory collections for the charities of our separated brothers. Charity is Christ's work and by taking a part in it wherever we find it, we testify to the world that we believe our charitable works to be done for Christ and within him. There is an altogether unwholesome competition in the area of charity; here we could well merge our efforts and as we grow in a

---

events, the service would be an extraordinary rite. But who could deny that, undertaken under the qualified conditions stated above, it would be a moving plea for unitive grace?

[2] A good example of such limited participation recently took place in Germany. A small group of Catholics and Protestants who spent some days together in prayer and discussion found a way of representing their basic unity in separation. On one day Catholics celebrated the Eucharist at which all were present, the Catholics forming an inner group and communicating, the Protestants forming an outer group and not communicating. On the next day there was a Lutheran celebration of the Lord's Supper with the groups reversed.

community of charitable works we would begin to see that we share a basic love for Christ that prompts these works. These limited exchanges would show us that even in our tragically fragmented state there is a community of faith, prayer, and charity that makes us basically one. The insight would sustain our determination to work harder for more comprehensive, visible unity.

Research Studies

But this interchurch participation cannot take place in a vacuum. There must be much more coming together in mutual respect to discuss the meaning and value of liturgy in the unitive life of the Church. We must undertake studies "in depth" aimed at tracing the rationale of Christian worship from its origin through its development in history. These studies would elucidate and work out scientifically a complete religious sociology, researching into the laws which determine collective human conduct in the worship life of Christians. This investigation would not be theoretical; it would look at the living history and at the psychology and conduct of nations and peoples in the concrete and seek to uncover the differing motives that account for our unhappy divisions. It would be hoped that in time principles would emerge upon which effective action for reunion could be based. There have been some beginnings in this area: our own Liturgical Conference is in communication with Protestant and Orthodox liturgists and the World Center for Liturgical Studies at Boca Raton, Florida, has been set up on an interchurch basis for mutual study of the liturgy and its unitive implications. Mr. Marshall has written on this point; he is a member of the World Center Board and can vouch for the good work that has begun there. The prospects for the future are most promising.

Liturgics, both Protestant and Catholic, is coming of age as a theological science. It would seem imperative that we exchange experts to conduct courses in our colleges and seminaries that aim at communicating to each other the rationale of our worship. Such courses would eliminate much of the subjective in our judgments about each other's worship. Young preachers and priests would enter on their ministerial life with mutual respect for the liturgy of their fellow Christians and be sympathetically appreciative of the distinctive elements of these liturgies which have heretofore not been appreciated or understood because they were viewed prejudicially and apart from a sincere rationale.

The Second Vatican Council has called for a complete renewal of the liturgy. In this effort it would seem wise for our liturgical scholars to consult the many learned Protestant scholars who head the liturgical commissions of the various denominations, federated church groups, and the World Council of Churches. Recent reformed Protestant liturgies bear the mark of solid liturgical scholarship; they claim Catholic elements as well as the best of the Reformed and Evangelical traditions (e.g., The Taizé Eucharistic Liturgy, The Liturgy of the Church of South India, The Evangelical Mass of the League for Evangelical-Catholic Reunion, the experimental liturgies from the Revision Commissions of the Church of England, etc.). These scholars have much to offer us; such interchurch consultation would doubtless provide rich ecumenical fruit.

Epilogue

We have spoken of the liturgy in its ideal expression as the instrument that shows forth and intensifies our unity in Christ. But the liturgy will accomplish its unitive purpose only when we participate in it knowingly and with fervor. The recent reforms, with promise of more to come, will make understanding and participation easier. But there must be a steady educational effort to make our people aware of the real meaning and demands of liturgy. For only when the liturgy in its external form mirrors a sincere interior liturgy of the soul, can it hope to serve as an efficacious means of unity among ourselves and be a source of communication between us and our Protestant brothers and thus bring us to a further degree of community.

Our people must be made aware that they worship because they are in truth the Church. The Church is not primarily a juridical entity—it is a worshiping fellowship formed by the Spirit of Christ for the sanctifying praise of a loving Father; it is the assembly of Christ wherein we find the saving Word of God, his grace and Sacraments. Our people must be taught that they worship together because, being many, they are one, and in order that they might be made more one. The unity that they see in the liturgy is the oneness that God wants for his people. In liturgy they reverence God as the Mystical Body of his Son; they perform that priestly office which Peter reminds us is the ". . . offering up of that spiritual sacrifice which God accepts through Jesus Christ" (I Pet 2:5). Liturgists and pastors can be thankful for external reforms, but they can never be satisfied until the faithful at Mass see these reforms as more meaningful external expressions of an interior renewal and conviction, which wells from a soul that has actually "experienced" and seeks to testify to its community in Christ.

Interior awareness therefore must accompany our adoption of present and future reforms. What we do we must do consciously and with understanding of the theological implications. But liturgy requires more than understanding. Scripture tells us that sincere prayer demands that our fervor and understanding be rooted in charity. We are told that before we approach God we must make sure that there is fraternal love in our hearts. Almost from the start of Christian history a lack of charity marred the unity of the Church. We know that the Christians of Corinth violated the liturgy of the "breaking of the bread" by their manifest lack of charity toward the poor (I Cor 11:17 ff). They failed to distinguish the uniqueness of the sacred meal which signified not just common eating and drinking but a joining with the brethren in the meal of Christ wherein he himself in his Body and Blood declared and intensified his oneness with us. Many ate but did not really unite themselves in love with the brethren and by not loving them showed what little love they had for Christ. Certainly in the subsequent divisions of Christians, particularly between Catholics and Protestants, no one can deny that countless sins against charity initiated and compounded our divisions. And who can deny that smallness, bigotry, and subtle and open forms of hatred still exist and harden us in our divisions? Certainly no one can fail to see the terrible scandal that our lack of genuine love for each other provides the "outsider," who sees the treatment we give each other proof enough for the validity of his judgment of the 'irrelevancy" of the Christian faith. But if our history has been marred by bitter divisions, we can begin to undo our divisions by manifesting a charity toward each other that is real and which finds its theological base in the belief that we share a community of grace with each other in Christ (even though our community is terribly fragmented in its visible effects). We should express this charity by genuine fraternity in our day to day contacts, by serious efforts to understand one another, to see and appreciate the viewpoint and beliefs of our fellow Christians. Above all we must cease to contemn the beliefs and worship of our brother Christians, even when these appear so very different from our own. The greatest charity we can extend our fellow Christians is a genuine respect for their faith and conscience. Sincere faith and conscience, after all, are the graces that God gives us to enable us to do his will.

Liturgy can strike its unitive fire within us when we come to it with love for the full brotherhood of Christ. When the liturgy is prayed in the spirit of fraternal love it can become our most effective prayer for unity. Paul exhorts Christians to remember:

> As God's chosen people, holy and well beloved, you must clothe yourselves with sentiments of compassion, kindness, humility, gentleness and patience. Bear with one another and forgive whatever grievances you have against each other. Just as the Lord has forgiven you, so you must forgive. But over all these virtues CLOTHE YOURSELVES WITH LOVE; IT IS THE BOND THAT PERFECTS AND BINDS US TOGETHER. Let the ruling principle of your hearts be the peace of Christ, to which you were called as members of one body, and be thankful. (Col 3:12-15)

If we had each of us kept even a minimum of fraternal love in our discussions, thoughts, and actions, we would never have created the deep divisions that separate us. And if divisions are to be repaired we must work to restore this fraternal love. Our long separatism makes this restoration difficult, but Christ has pledged his help to see us united in love. He prayed that we might be united in the same way that he was united in love with his Father. "May the love with which you love me dwell in them as I dwell in them myself." (Jo 17:26) May Christians sincerely join Christ in that prayer daily, for in a prayer life permeated with love for God and man lies our ultimate hope for Christian unity.

Bibliographies

General Protestant Bibliography

Abba, Raymond, *Principles of Christian Worship* (London: Oxford University Press, 1957).

Aulén, Gustaf, *Eucharist and Sacrifice,* Eric H. Whalstrom, trans. (Philadelphia: Muhlenberg Press, 1958).

Baillie, Donald M., *The Theology of the Sacraments* (New York: Charles Scribner's Sons, 1957).

Bishop, John, *Methodist Worship in Relation to Free Church Worship* (London: Epworth Press, 1950).

The Book of Common Worship (Philadelphia: Board of Christian Education of the Presbyterian Church in the U.S.A., 1956).

Book of Worship, approved by the General Synod of the Evangelical and Reformed Church (St. Louis: Eden Publishing House, 1947).

Bowmer, J. C., *Sacrament of the Lord's Supper in Early Methodism* (London: Dacre Press, 1950).

Brenner, Scott F., *The Art of Worship* (New York: The Macmillan Company, 1961).

———, *The Way of Worship* (New York: The Macmillan Company, 1944).

———, and others, *A Handbook of Worship* (Philadelphia: Heidelberg Press, 1958).

Brilioth, Yngve, *Eucharistic Faith and Practice: Evangelical and Catholic* (London: S.P.C.K., 1930).

Cirlot, F. L., *The Early Eucharist* (London: S.P.C.K., 1939).

Coffin, Henry S., *The Public Worship of God* (Philadelphia: The Westminster Press, 1946).

Cullmann, Oscar, *Early Christian Worship* (London: S.C.M. Press, 1953).

———, and F. J. Leenhardt, *Essays on the Lord's Supper* (Richmond, Va.: John Knox Press, 1958).

Davies, Horton, *The Worship of the English Puritans* (London: Dacre Press, 1948).

De Candole, Henry, *The Church's Offering* (London: A. R. Mowbray & Company, Ltd., 1951).

Dix, Gregory, *The Shape of the Liturgy* (London: Dacre Press, 1945).

Dodd, C. H., *Apostolic Preaching* (London: Hodder and Stoughton, 1936).

Duchesne, Louis, *Christian Worship: Its Origins and Evolution* (New York: The Macmillan Company, 1931).

Dunkle, William F., *Values in the Church Year* (Nashville, Tenn.: Abingdon Press, 1959).

Dunlop, Colin, *Anglican Public Worship* (London: S.C.M. Press, 1953).

Edwall, Pehr, Eric Hayman, and William D. Maxwell, eds., *Ways of Worship* (New York: Harper & Row, Publishers, 1951).

Fey, Harold E., *The Lord's Supper: Seven Meanings* (New York: Harper & Row, Publishers, 1948).

Forsyth, P. T., *The Church and the Sacraments* (London: Independent Press, Ltd., 1955).

Frere, Walter H., *The Anaphora, or Great Eucharistic Prayer* (New York: The Macmillan Company, 1938).

Garrett, T. S., *The Liturgy of the Church of South India* (London: Oxford University Press, 1954).

Gibson, G. M., *The Story of the Christian Year* (Nashville, Tenn.: Abingdon Press, 1945).

Hardon, John A., *The Protestant Churches of America* (Westminster, Md.: The Newman Press, 1956).

Hebert, A. G., *The Parish Communion* (New York: The Macmillan Company, 1937).

Hedley, George, *Christian Worship* (New York: The Macmillan Company, 1953).

Herbert, A. S., *Worship in Ancient Israel* (Richmond, Va.: John Knox Press, 1959).

Hislop, D. H., *Our Heritage in Public Worship* (New York: Charles Scribner's Sons, 1935).

Horton, Douglas, *The Meaning of Worship* (New York: Harper & Row, Publishers, 1959).

Horton, Walter M., *Our Christian Faith, Congregationalism Today and Tomorrow* (Boston: Pilgrim Press, 1954).

Hurlbut, Stephen A., *The Liturgy of the Church of Scotland since the Reformation* (Charleston: St. Alban's Press, 1950).

Jones, Illion T., *A Historical Approach to Evangelical Worship* (Nashville, Tenn.: Abingdon Press, 1954).

Kerr, Hugh T., *The Christian Sacraments* (Philadelphia: The Westminster Press, 1944).

The Lord's Supper, A Baptist Statement (London: Carey Kingsgate Press, 1955).

Lowrie, Walter, *Action in the Liturgy: Essential and Unessential* (New York: Philosophical Library, 1953).

The Lutheran Liturgy (Philadelphia: Muhlenberg Press, 1949).

MacGregor, Geddes, *The Coming Reformation* (Philadelphia: The Westminster Press, 1960).

Mascall, E. L., *Corpus Christi* (New York: Longmans Green & Co., Inc., 1955).

Maxwell, William D., *Concerning Worship* (London: Oxford University Press, 1958).

———, *John Knox's Genevan Service Book* (Edinburgh: Oliver and Boyd, 1931).

———, *An Outline of Christian Worship* (London: Oxford University Press, 1948).

Micklem, Nathaniel, ed., *Christian Worship* (New York: Oxford University Press, 1936).

Minchin, Basil, *Covenant and Sacrifice* (New York: Longmans Green & Co., Inc., 1958).

Nash, Arnold S., ed., *Protestant Thought in the Twentieth Century* (New York: The Macmillan Company, 1951).

Nicholls, William, *Jacob's Ladder: The Meaning of Worship* (Richmond, Va.: John Knox Press, 1958).

Oesterly, W. O. E., *The Jewish Background of the Christian Liturgy* (London: Oxford University Press, 1925).

Otto, Rudolph, *The Idea of the Holy* (New York: Oxford University Press, 1925).

Oulton, J. E. L., *Holy Communion and the Holy Spirit* (London: S.P.C.K., 1951).

Payne, E. A., *The Fellowship of Believers* (London: Carey Kingsgate Press, 1954).

Piepkorn, Arthur C., *Worship and the Sacraments* (St. Louis: Concordia Publishing House, 1952).

Rattenbury, J., *The Eucharistic Hymns of John and Charles Wesley* (London: Epworth Press, 1948).

Reed, Luther D., *The Lutheran Liturgy* (Philadelphia: Muhlenberg Press, 1949).

Shands, Alfred R., *The Liturgical Movement and the Local Church* (London: S.C.M. Press, 1959).

Shepherd, Massey H., *The Liturgy and the Christian Faith* (Greenwich, Conn.: The Seabury Press, Inc., 1957).

———, *Paschal Liturgy and the Apocalypse* (Richmond, Va.: John Knox Press, 1960).

———, ed., *The Eucharist and the Liturgical Renewal* (New York: Oxford University Press, 1960).

———, ed., *The Liturgical Renewal of the Church* (New York: Oxford University Press, 1960).

———, *The Living Liturgy* (New York: Oxford University Press, 1946).

Sperry, Willard C., *Reality in Worship* (New York: The Macmillan Company, 1925).

Strawley, J. H., *The Early History of the Liturgy* (New York: The Macmillan Company, 1956).

Strodach, Paul Z., *A Manual on Worship* (Philadelphia: Muhlenberg Press, 1930).

Sweet, William, *Methodism in American History* (Nashville, Tenn.: Abingdon Press, 1953).

Thurian, Max, *The Eucharistic Memorial,* J. G. Davies, trans., in two vols. (Richmond, Va.: John Knox Press, 1960-61).

Underhill, Evelyn, *Worship* (New York: Harper & Row, Publishers, 1937).

Vajta, Vilmos, *Luther on Worship,* U.S. Leupold, trans. (Philadelphia: Muhlenberg Press, 1958).

Vogt, Von Ogden, *Art and Religion* (Boston: Beacon Press, 1948).

Wedel, Theodore O., *The Coming Great Church* (New York: The Macmillan Company, 1945).

Weigel, Gustave, *Survey of Protestant Theology in Our Day* (Westminster, Md.: The Newman Press, 1954).

White, James F., H. Grady Hardin, and Joseph D. Quillian, Jr., *The Celebration of the Gospel* (Nashville, Tenn.: Abingdon Press, 1964).

Williams, J. Paul, *What Americans Believe and How They Worship* (New York: Harper & Row, Publishers, 1952).

General Catholic Bibliography

Adam, Karl, *Christ Our Brother* (New York: Sheed & Ward, 1931).

Assisi Papers (Collegeville, Minn.: The Liturgical Press, 1957).

Beauduin, Lambert, *Liturgy, the Life of the Church* (Collegeville, Minn.: The Liturgical Press, 1929).

Bouyer, Louis, *Liturgical Piety* (Notre Dame, Ind.: University of Notre Dame Press, 1955).

———, *The Paschal Mystery* (Chicago: Henry Regnery Co., 1950).

———, *The Spirit and Forms of Protestantism,* A. W. Littledale, trans. (Westminster, Md.: The Newman Press, 1957).

———, *The Word, the Church and the Sacraments in Catholicism and Protestantism* (New York: Desclée Co., Inc., 1961).

Casel, Odo, *The Mystery of Christian Worship* (Westminster, Md.: The Newman Press, 1962).

Chevrot, Georges, *Our Mass* (Tenbury Wells, Worc., England: Challoner Publications, Ltd., 1958).

Congar, Yves, *Lay People in the Church* (Westminster, Md.: The Newman Press, 1957).

———, *The Mystery of the Church* (Baltimore: Helicon Press, Inc., 1960).

Constitution on the Sacred Liturgy of the Second Vatican Council, The (Rome: Paulist Press Edition, 1964).

Dalmais, I. H., *Introduction to the Liturgy* (Baltimore: Helicon Press, Inc., 1961).

Danielou, Jean, *The Bible and the Liturgy* (Notre Dame, Ind.: University of Notre Dame Press, 1956).

Davis, Charles, *Liturgy and Doctrine* (New York: Sheed & Ward, 1960).

Delorme, J., P. Benoit, and others, *The Eucharist in the New Testament* (Baltimore: Helicon Press, Inc., 1964).

Diekmann, Godfrey, *Come Let Us Worship* (Baltimore: Helicon Press, Inc., 1961).

Durrwell, Francis X., *The Resurrection* (New York: Sheed & Ward, 1960).

Ellard, Gerald, *Christian Life and Worship* (Milwaukee: Bruce Publishing Co., 1941).

———, *The Mass in Transition* (Milwaukee: Bruce Publishing Co., 1956).

———, *The Mass of the Future* (Milwaukee: Bruce Publishing Co., 1948).

d' Eypernon, Taymans, *The Blessed Trinity and the Sacraments* (Westminster, Md.: The Newman Press, 1961).

Guardini, Romano, *The Spirit of the Liturgy* (New York: Sheed & Ward, 1953).

Hastings, Cecily, *The Sacraments* (New York: Sheed & Ward, 1961).

Henry, Antoine, ed., *Christ in His Sacraments* (Notre Dame, Ind.: Fides Publishers Assn., 1958).

Hofinger, Johannes, ed., *Liturgy and the Missions* (Collegeville, Minn.: The Liturgical Press, 1962).

Hogan, William F., *Christ's Redemptive Sacrifice* (Englewood Cliffs, N.J.: Prentice-Hall, Inc., 1963).

Hovda, Robert W., ed., *Sunday Morning Crisis* (Baltimore: Helicon Press, Inc., 1963).

Howell, Clifford, *Of Sacraments and Sacrifice* (Collegeville, Minn.: The Liturgical Press, 1952).

Jungmann, J. A., *The Early Liturgy* (Notre Dame, Ind.: University of Notre Dame Press, 1959).

———, *Liturgical Worship* (New York: Frederick Pustet Co., Inc., 1941).

———, *The Mass of the Roman Rite*, 2 Vols. (New York: Benziger Brothers, Inc., 1951).

———, *Pastoral Liturgy* (New York: Herder & Herder, Inc., 1962).

———, *The Sacrament of the Church: The Meaning of the Mass,* Clifford Howell, trans. (Collegeville, Minn.: The Liturgical Press, 1955).

———, *The Sacrifice of the Church* (Collegeville, Minn.: The Liturgical Press, 1956).

King, James W., *Liturgy and the Laity* (Westminster, Md.: The Newman Press, 1963).

Leeming, Bernard, *Principles of Sacramental Theology* (Westminster, Md.: The Newman Press, 1960).

Liturgy and the Word of God, The, The Strasbourg Papers (Collegeville, Minn.: The Liturgical Press, 1959).

Louvel, F., and L. J. Putz, *Signs of Life* (Notre Dame, Ind.: Fides Publishers Assn., 1953).

de Lubac, Henri, *Catholicism* (New York: Longmans, Green & Co., 1950).

Martimort, Aimé G., *In Remembrance of Me* (Collegeville, Minn.: The Liturgical Press, 1958).

———, *The Signs of the New Covenant* (Collegeville, Minn.: The Liturgical Press, 1963).

Masure, Eugene, *The Christian Sacrifice* (New York: P. J. Kenedy & Sons, 1943).

———, *The Sacrifice of the Mystical Body* (Chicago: Henry Regnery Co., 1958).

Mersch, Emile, *The Theology of the Mystical Body* (St. Louis: B. Herder Book Co., 1951).

Miller, John H., *Signs of Transformation in Christ* (Englewood Cliffs, N.J.: Prentice-Hall, Inc., 1963).

Nocent, Adrian, *The Future of the Liturgy* (New York: Herder & Herder, Inc., 1963).

Palmer, Paul F., *Sacraments and Worship, Sources of Christian Theology,* Vol. I (Westminster, Md.: The Newman Press, 1955).

Parsch, Pius, *The Church's Year of Grace,* 5 Vols. (Collegeville, Minn.: The Liturgical Press, 1953-62).

———, *The Liturgy of the Mass* (St. Louis: B. Herder Book Co., 1941).

Pius XII, *Mediator Dei,* Encyclical on the Sacred Liturgy (Rome: America Press Edition, 1947).

———, *Mystici Corporis,* Encyclical on the Mystical Body of Christ (Rome: America Press Edition, 1943).

Rahner, Karl, *The Church and the Sacraments* (New York: Herder & Herder, Inc., 1963).

Reinhold, H. A., *Bringing the Mass to the People* (Baltimore: Helicon Press, Inc., 1960).

———, *The Dynamics of the Liturgy* (New York: The Macmillan Company, 1961).

Roguet, A. M., *Christ Acts Through Sacraments* (Collegeville, Minn.: The Liturgical Press, 1954).

———, *Holy Mass* (London: Blackfriars Publications, 1953).

Scheeben, Matthias J., *The Mysteries of Christianity* (St. Louis: B. Herder Book Co., 1946).

Schillebeeckx, Edouard, *Christ the Sacrament of the Encounter with God* (New York: Sheed & Ward, 1963).

Sullivan, C. Stephen, *Readings in Sacramental Theology* (Englewood Cliffs, N.J.: Prentice-Hall, Inc., 1964).

de la Taille, Maurice, *The Mystery of the Faith* (New York: Sheed & Ward, 1940).

Vagaggini, Cyprian, *Theological Dimensions of the Liturgy* (Collegeville, Minn.: The Liturgical Press, 1959).

Vonier, Anscar, *A Key to the Doctrine of the Eucharist* (Westminster, Md.: The Newman Press, 1948).

Ecumenical Literature: A Protestant Bibliography

Benoit, J. D., *Liturgical Renewal: Studies in Catholic and Protestant Developments on the Continent* (London: S.C.M. Press, 1958).

Bradshaw, Marion J., *Free Churches and Church Unity* (Boston: Beacon Press, 1954).

Cavert, Samuel McCrea, *On the Road to Christian Unity* (New York: Harper & Row, Publishers, 1961).

Craig, Clarence Tucker, *One Church in the Light of the New Testament* (Nashville, Tenn.: Abingdon Press, 1951).

Cullmann, Oscar, *Message to Catholics and Protestants* (Grand Rapids, Mich.: Wm. B. Eerdmans, 1959).

Garrison, Winfred E., *Christian Unity and the Disciples of Christ* (St. Louis, Mo.: The Bethany Press, 1955).

———, *The Quest and Character of a United Church* (Nashville, Tenn.: Abingdon Press, 1957).

Horton, Walter M., *Christian Theology: an Ecumenical Approach*, Rev. Ed. (New York: The Macmillan Company, 1958).

Hunt, George L., *Guide to Christian Unity* (St. Louis, Mo.: The Bethany Press, 1958).

Mascall, E. L., *The Recovery of Unity* (London: Longmans, Green & Co., 1958).

Minear, Paul S., *Nature of the Unity We Seek* (St. Louis, Mo.: The Bethany Press, 1958).

Kean, Charles Duell, *Road to Reunion* (Greenwich, Conn.: The Seabury Press, Inc., 1958).

Neill, Stephen C., *Brothers of the Faith* (Nashville, Tenn.: Abingdon Press, 1960).

Nelson, J. Robert, *One Lord, One Church* (New York: Association Press, 1958).

Nelson, Robert J., *Christian Unity in North America* (St. Louis: The Bethany Press, 1958).

Outler, A. C., *Christian Tradition and the Unity We Seek* (New York: Oxford University Press, 1957).

Pittenger, Norman, *The Church, the Ministry, and Reunion* (Greenwich, Conn.: The Seabury Press, Inc., 1957).

Rouse, Ruth, and Stephen Charles Neill, eds., *History of the Ecumenical Movement, 1517-1948* (Philadelphia: The Westminster Press, 1954).

Schutz, Roger, *Unity: Man's Tomorrow* (New York: Herder & Herder, Inc., 1962).

Spinka, Matthew, *The Quest for Christian Unity* (New York: The Macmillan Company, 1960).

Subilia, Vittorio, *The Problem of Catholicism* (Philadelphia: The Westminister Press, 1964).

Thurian, Max, *Visible Unity and Tradition* (Baltimore: Helicon Press, Inc., 1962).

Visser 't Hooft, W. A., *The Renewal of the Church* (London: S.C.M. Press, 1956).

Ecumenical Literature: A Catholic Bibliography[1]

Baum, Gregory, *That They May Be One* (Westminster, Md.: The Newman Press, 1958).

———, *Progress and Perspectives* (New York: Sheed & Ward, 1962).

Bea, Augustin Cardinal, *The Unity of Christians* (New York: Herder & Herder, Inc., 1963).

Boyer, Charles, *Christian Unity* (New York: Hawthorn Books, Inc., 1962).

Congar, Yves, *Divided Christendom* (London: Geoffrey Bles, Ltd., Publishers, 1939).

Dumont, Christophe, *Approaches to Christian Unity* (Baltimore: Helicon Press, Inc., 1959).

Hardon, John A., *Christianity in Conflict* (Westminster, Md.: The Newman Press, 1959).

Heenan John, ed., *Christian Unity: A Catholic View* (London: Sheed & Ward, 1962).

Küng, Hans, *The Council, Reform and Reunion* (New York: Sheed & Ward, 1961).

Leeming, Bernard, *The Churches and the Church* (Westminster, Md.: The Newman Press, 1960).

McNally, Robert, *Reform of the Church* (New York: Herder & Herder, Inc., 1963).

[1] This and the inter-church bibliography that follows are by no means exhaustive; they list works on the ecumenical movement which have been written or translated into English.

McNamara, Kevin, ed., *Christian Unity* (Maynooth, Ireland, 1962).

North American Liturgical Week, *The Liturgy and Unity in Christ* (Washington: The Liturgical Conference, 1961).

St. John, Henry, *Essays in Christian Unity 1928-1954* (Westminster, Md.: The Newman Press, 1955).

Sartory, Thomas, *The Oecumenical Movement and the Unity of the Church* (Oxford, Eng.: Basil Blackwell & Mott, Ltd., 1963).

Swidler, Leonard, ed., *Dialogue for Reunion* (New York: Herder & Herder, Inc., 1962).

Tavard, Georges, *The Catholic Approach to Protestantism* (New York: Harper & Row, Publishers, 1955).

———, *Protestant Hopes and Catholic Responsibility* (Notre Dame, Ind.: Fides Publishers Assn., 1960).

———, *Protestantism* (New York: Hawthorn Books, Inc., 1959).

———, *Two Centuries of Ecumenism* (Notre Dame, Ind.: Fides Publishers Assn., 1960).

Taylor, Michael J., *The Protestant Liturgical Renewal* (Westminster, Md.: The Newman Press, 1963).

Todd, John, *Catholicism and the Ecumenical Movement* (London: Longmans Green & Co., 1956).

Villain, Maurice, *Unity* (London: The Harvill Press Ltd., 1963).

Weigel, Gustave, *A Catholic Primer on the Ecumenical Movement* (Westminster, Md.: The Newman Press, 1958).

———, *Catholic Theology in Dialogue* (New York: Harper & Row, Publishers, 1961).

———, *Faith and Understanding in America* (New York: The Macmillan Company, 1959).

Willebrands, and others, *Problems Before Unity* (Baltimore: Helicon Press, Inc., 1962).

Ecumenical Literature: Inter-Church Symposia

Asmussen, Hans, and Thomas Sartory, *Lutheran-Catholic: Unity?* (Baltimore: Helicon Press, Inc., 1960).

Bevan, R. J., ed., *The Churches and Christian Unity* (London: Oxford University Press, 1963).

Bosc, J., J. Guitton, and J. Danielou, *The Catholic Protestant Dialogue* (Baltimore: Helicon Press, Inc., 1960).

Brown, Robert McAfee, and Gustave Weigel, *An American Dialogue* (New York: Doubleday & Company, Inc., 1960).

Callahan Daniel, ed., *Christianity Divided* (New York: Sheed & Ward, 1961).

Christians in Conversation, papers of a colloquy held at St. John's Abbey, Collegeville, Minn., 1961, organized by the American Benedictine Academy (Westminster, Md.: The Newman Press, 1962).

Cowan, Wayne, ed., *Facing Protestant-Roman Catholic Tensions* (New York: Association Press, 1960).

Cristiani, L., and J. Rilliet, *Catholics and Protestants: Separated Brothers* (Westminster, Md.: The Newman Press, 1960).

Morris, William, ed., *The Unity We Seek* (Toronto: Ryerson Press, 1962).

Scharper, Philip, ed., *American Catholics: a Protestant-Jewish View* (New York: Sheed & Ward, 1959).

Marshall S.J. and Taylor S.J.

AUTHOR

Liturgy & Christian Unity

TITLE

DATE DUE	BORROWER'S NAME	ROOM NUMBER
7/30/65	Norma La Fond	256
8/6/65	Jerry Modrell	246
8/13/65	Esther Scherman	252
11/19/71	Rick Coleen St.